Growing Up
Church of Christ

Mike S. Allen

ISBN: 0615514812
ISBN-13: 978-0615514819

Book design by Johnny Flash Productions.

Author's Note

I began writing this sort-of memoir in the winter of 2009, but it really existed long before that. It sat in journals and in photo albums and on random pieces of paper in shoeboxes. I wanted to pull together the bits and pieces of my story—of growing up in the Church of Christ, and I wanted to hear other people's stories as well. So I asked some old friends and friends-of-old friends for their two cents, and many obliged.

Thanks to everyone who shared or who considered sharing. There were certainly some nice surprises along the way.

You'll see people's names and years of birth in here. I thought this might give some context to what we were all saying. Some of the names and personal details have been changed to protect privacy, but the stories are true and real. At least they are as true and real as our memories allow. You'll also see the "church" part of Church of Christ capitalized sometimes and not capitalized at other times. Different people wrote it different ways, and I mostly just left it as it was. No offense is intended either way.

By the time you make it to "The End," I hope you'll have found a connection to some thought or story, and in that connection, I hope you will have been helped a little in your own journey.

Best wishes always,
Mike (b. 1966)

CONTENTS

AT CAMP

AT SCHOOL

LIFE AND DOCTRINE

LATER ON

For my wife Cheryl, a beautiful poet.

GROWING UP CHURCH OF CHRIST

A Little Background

The Church of Christ emerged from what's been called the Restoration Movement of the early- to mid-1800s. The founding fathers of this movement wanted to move churches back to the Christian ideal, a New Testament church that was closely modeled after the churches of the first century A.D. It was a noble undertaking. The number one guy, sort of the George Washington of the Church of Christ, was Alexander Campbell. He was widely known for saying that Christians should speak where the Bible speaks and be silent where the Bible is silent. This phrase influenced a strong adherence to scriptures among members of the Churches of Christ.

Now, fast forward about a hundred years to the Church of Christ of the 1970s and 80s, the church where I grew up. Here were some of the practices that made us different from other types of churches:

- Baptism, a complete immersion in water, was a big deal. A person was considered "saved" at the point of baptism.

- Communion (a.k.a. the Lord's Supper) was taken by a congregation every Sunday.

• Women were not allowed to hold positions in the church which would place them in authority over men. Women could not lead in public worship.

• Instrumental music was considered a no-no. In some churches, this included music for weddings, funerals, etc. All singing was performed a cappella.

• Typically, church services were held 3 times a week— Sunday morning, Sunday night, and Wednesday night. Members were expected to attend all 3 services.

• Certain outside-of-church actions were frowned upon. These activities included drinking alcohol, dancing, and mixed swimming.

Early On

In the Beginning

I was born in Searcy, Arkansas on a cold Monday afternoon in February 1966. Actually, I don't remember if it was
cold. I'm just guessing.

I am the son of Jimmy Allen, a famous Church of Christ
preacher, and of Marilyn Allen, a not-so-famous Church of
Christ Bible class teacher.

I am the younger brother of Cindy (a.k.a. Cindy Lynn or
Sis) and Jimmy (a.k.a. Little Jimmy or Jimbo).

Little Jimmy would grow up to become a Church of
Christ preacher. Cindy would grow up to marry a Church
of Christ preacher.

But what would become of me?

My Earliest Memories

At the dawn of my life, I remember going to church, going to Bible class, going to vacation Bible school, going to gospel meetings, having family devotionals, praying before meals, praying before bedtime, memorizing scriptures, listening to Bible stories, and going to church potlucks.

Our family was busy for the Lord.

————

The first preacher I knew at the College Church of Christ was Al Jolly.

How could you not like a man named Brother Jolly?

————

The sound man.

The sound man worked at the back of the auditorium near a large plywood cabinet. He turned dials inside the cabinet to adjust the pulpit microphone volume. He pressed the RECORD button to tape the sermons.

The sound man sat on a big chair with thick cushions.

Why did he get to relax on a padded chair while the rest of us were sitting on hard wooden pews? Who did he think he was, the King of Siam or something?

————

Sunday morning announcement:

"We have a cry room located at the rear of the auditorium..."

(The man at the microphone raises his right arm, palm slightly turned upward, and points toward the back.)

"...for nursing mothers and for mothers of young children."

The cry room.

Dimmed lights.

Tinted glass in the front.

Brown-boxed speaker hanging on the wall.

Babies feeding, and toddlers in sock-feet crawling on the floor.

Picture books passing back and forth.

Moms exchanging whispers and warm glances and occasional giggles.

Things getting a bit unruly at times.

———

In my pre-school years, I had a recurring nightmare.

I dreamed about a pitch black sky and a little red man with horns. The man was far away from me, crouched down and smiling. After a little while, he would start running toward me, growing bigger and bigger. I would stand watching him, unable to move a muscle or even speak.

When the man got close, I'd wake up, my heart beating out of my chest.

———

LITTLE MIKE: What's your favorite color, Dad?

DAD: Well, I'd probably have to say red, because it reminds me of the blood that Jesus shed for us on the cross.

That was all I needed to hear. Red would be my favorite color too.

———

"You're a fool!"

That's what I told Dad's friend while we were all fishing. He had just done something foolish, and I called him out. With a smile on my face, I said, "You are a fool."

"Hey, boy. What did you just say?"

That was the voice of my dad.

I zipped my lips.

"You are never to say that again. Do you understand me? Jesus told us, if you call someone a fool…"

(Dad was in sermon-mode now.)

"… then you are in danger of hell fire. You cannot call someone a fool."

I got the message, and I tried my best to stop saying that word. I really did. But sometimes it would sneak out, like my mouth had a mind of its own. And when Dad heard about it...

Whack. Whack. Whack.

(For those of you who might not understand this part—like maybe if you grew up somewhere in the North and had very liberal parents—"whack" is the sound of a big ol' calloused hand hitting the backside of some cutoff blue jeans.)

Sometime later, my brother Jimmy and I were playing Nerf hoops in my bedroom. He made me mad, and I said, "YOU FOOL!"

Jimmy stopped the game and told me to go see Dad and confess. I didn't want to go, but I did.

Whack. Whack. Whack.

I decided to stop calling people fools.

————

At the end of a family devotional, we'd gather in the center of the living room, holding hands in a circle. I'd stare down at everyone's feet, checking out the different colored socks and my dad's thick toenails. Someone would start singing:

Blest be the tie that binds…

And we'd all join in.

Our hearts in Christian love;
The fellowship of kindred minds
Is like to that above.

There was warmth in that circle. And maybe a little glimpse of heaven? Would that be saying too much?

At Church

Three Times a Week

Most Churches of Christ held worship services (and/or Bible classes) three times a week: Sunday morning, Sunday evening, and Wednesday night.

———

We played in Harding Park on Sunday afternoons. War games or sports games. Running around in the wide open spaces with the other kids from the neighborhoods. Sweating and yelling like crazy.

At about 3:30, moms would stick their heads out of doors, calling for their boys and girls to come home and get ready for the 4:00 church service. The park would be mostly deserted after that.

On one afternoon when the calls came, I decided not to run home. Not at 3:30 or 4:30 or even 5:30. I just put my head down and kept on playing. I was having too much fun. I would have kept on going too, right through the "late service"—the 6:00 evening worship service—if Dad hadn't driven over to the park to find me ... if he hadn't rolled down the window of our car and shouted, "Hey, boy, hop in! We're going to church!"

Yeah, if Dad hadn't come by and picked me up, I might still be playing in the park right now.

I told a Catholic friend about my church.

He laughed, "You go to church three times a week? Are you kidding?"

Somewhere along the way, I heard the nickname "SMO" (rhymes with "snow"). It was used to describe someone who came to church on Sunday Mornings Only.

Elisabeth (b. 193X)

My husband's health is not good now, but he still attends elders meetings and church services. Sometimes I feel that we should stay home and rest on Sunday nights, but he never permits such a thing. So we go, even when we are tired, and I always come home feeling better.

Michael (b. 1963)

Everyone dressed up for Sunday morning church. On Sunday night and Wednesday night, you could wear your school clothes.

Phil (b. 1956)

I faked being sick sometimes so I could skip the Sunday

night service.

Kevin (b. 1966)

Until my early 20s, I really didn't have a personal relationship with Christ, and it didn't bother me much because I never "forsook the assembly."

Small Churches

The College Church, the church I attended in Searcy for the first 23 years of my life, was huge. I'm pretty sure there were well over a thousand members there. But in the surrounding cities and counties, the churches were often much smaller.

From time to time, our family would visit these smaller congregations, especially if my dad or brother or brother-in-law was preaching. One Sunday morning, we attended a church with less than 10 members. The members sat on the left side of the auditorium, and my family sat on the right.

———

Signs by the side of the road. Small signs that say CHURCH of CHRIST 1.5 miles and an arrow pointing to the right or left. Riding in the car with my dad. Going fishing and watching the signs. Windows rolled down. Warm air blowing across our faces. Herb Alpert & The Tijuana Brass playing on the radio. Cruising down an old highway with soybean fields flying past on both sides. Passing through Arkansas backwater towns—Judsonia, Possum Grape, Olyphant—on a lazy summer day.

———

Elizabeth (b. 196X)

I attended a small Spanish-speaking church until I was about 16 years old. My mom taught Bible classes there, and my dad always led singing. Sometimes the services would last forever because the announcements portion would turn into a congregation discussion time. I knew a lot more details about those people's lives than any young person really needed to know.

The Worship Service

The church met for worship service for about an hour and a quarter on Sunday mornings and for about an hour on Sunday evenings.

———

A typical Sunday morning service might run something like this:

Announcements (for upcoming weddings, funerals, etc.)

Opening prayer (often beginning with the phrase, "Let us pray...")

A few songs (for clarity, songs numbers would be said twice, like this: "Please turn to song number three hundred ninety-three. Number three, nine, three")

Another prayer

A couple more songs

Communion (scripture and prayer for the "bread," followed by a prayer for the "fruit of the vine")

Prayer for the contribution (sometimes with the comment, "Separate and apart from the Lord's Supper, we now take our weekly offering")

A song

The sermon

An invitation song (and, if people responded, reading of the names and of respondee comments, followed by a prayer and then baptisms, if applicable

Another song

Closing prayer

––––––––

Sunday morning worship service. Feeling hot and bothered. 6-year-old me squirming on a wooden pew between my mom and a stack of books. Sitting on the far right side of the balcony. Second row by the window. In the summer, I could push the pane open a little bit and see an occasional car going past on the side street. Oh to be in that car! Riding free with the windows rolled down! Anything to be out of this boring old church service.

No thanks, mom, I don't want to look at another picture book.

If I got too squirmy, mom would drag me down the stairs from the balcony, holding me by the wrist and not by the hand. She'd take me outside and threaten a spanking. I wouldn't necessarily get a spanking. I'd just get threatened with one. And we were outside, which was nice. But it could be kind of embarrassing too, especially if the men waiting in the back lobby to serve communion saw us.

I'd tell Mom that I'd do better. I'd listen. I'd be quiet. I'd be good. I'd act just the way she wanted. But it wouldn't last. I'd be back outside again on another Sunday morning, trying to talk myself out of a spanking.

———

When our family got back to the car after church, my brother said, "Brother C's prayer lasted 8 minutes. I timed it on my watch."

8 minutes! Now, we had men at the College Church who could go for maybe 5 minutes, but no one was in Brother C's league. 8 minutes! That's a lifetime to kid.

From the time he said, "Our holy Father who art in heaven...

> *if I wanted to,*
> *I could walk across the street,*
> *buy and eat a box of Cracker Jacks,*
> *and make it back into the auditorium,*
> *before Brother C said,*

... We pray all of these things in Christ our loving savior's name, amen."

His prayers were full of Thees and Thous, and sometimes I had a hard time understanding them. But they did sound pretty good. I'll give that to Brother C; they had sort of a psalm-like quality about them.

They were beautiful prayers.

And they were looooooong.

———

Kim (b. 1979)

Taking communion, every single week, has been very meaningful to me.

Cheryl (b. 1967)

When we were kids, my friend Michele and I would draw pictures during church service. We'd sketch girls wearing beauty pageant dresses and sashes and having gorgeous hair that came all the way down to their ankles.

Michael (b. 1963)

We sang the same songs and had the same number of songs. We heard the same prayers and had the same number of prayers. There was so much repetition.

Bible Class

At the College Church, we met in Bible classes by age, and later by school grade. Our weekly class times were 9:45 on Sunday morning and 7:00 on Wednesday evenings. From 5th grade until 8th grade or so, our class was divided into separate groups for girls and boys.

———

Memorizing scripture was important.

A teacher told us a story about some men who had been captured during a war. The men were held in a prison camp without any access to the Bible. All they could do was rely on scriptures they had learned in the past. And since they had done such a good job of learning verses when they were young, the men were able to piece together large chunks of God's word from their memories.

"Wasn't that a neat story, class?"

A neat story? I thought it was a scary story!

I did not want to grow up and go off to war and get captured and be placed in a prison camp where all of us POWs had to re-create the Bible based on scriptures we had memorized. I mostly wanted to just stay close to home and read books and eat chocolate chip cookies (with a cold glass of milk, please).

————

Mom taught our 3rd or 4th grade Wednesday night Bible class. She prepared for the class like crazy, planning craft activities, flannel board stories, memory verse posters, and film strip lessons. You name it, she did it. She even wrote weekly letters and mailed them to us. (Most of our parents were connected to Harding College, so the correspondence traveled through Campus Mail for free.) One of Mom's letters was written backwards, like a passage from Leonardo da Vinci's notebook, so we had to hold it up to a mirror to read it. That was kind of cool.

Later in the year, on a summer Wednesday night, Mom piled all of us into a couple of cars and took us over to her co-teacher's house. At the door, the robed co-teacher told us she was Lydia, seller of purple. Inside the home, the women served us a Bible meal—okay the lentils weren't so hot—and taught us the story of Lydia from a first-person perspective. It was an awesome night.

Can you imagine breaking out of Bible class for a field trip? The freedom of that?

————

In junior high, our classes met in a small house across the street from the main College Church building. The church had purchased the house because our congregation was growing, and we needed the extra space.

On Wednesday nights, most of the junior high crowd would hang out in front of the classroom-house, standing in the yard or leaning against cars in the driveway, killing time before the evening session started. Then, at 7:00, we'd wind down our conversations and slowly file up to the front door.

Our boys' class met in the very first room, what used to be the living room. Our chairs were spread in a loose semi-circle against three walls. The western wall was covered in windows, and in the summer, the shadows on the floor would grow like beanstalks as the sun went down.

Our group was a somewhat rowdy bunch, that was our reputation at least—a bright bunch of boys with too much energy buzzing around inside our bodies. Our teacher, Mr. D, was a middle-aged guy with a firm hand, but he still had some trouble controlling us.

One night, we seemed especially restless. Maybe there was a full moon. Although I was participating in the general ruckus, I began toning things down when Mr. D's eyes started to bulge. My friend Brad wasn't so good at the toning-down part. On this night, he sat across the room from me, bouncing up and down in his seat.

Mr. D's face was a mask of frustration. He was definitely approaching the point of can't-stand-this-nonsense-any-longer. Most of us had seen it before with other adults.

Then, as quickly as you could snap your fingers, Mr. D scurried across the room and aimed a karate kick at Brad's chest. It connected with a thud. Brad stopped his bouncing, and his face turned completely red. I thought he was going to cry, and some of the boys around him giggled nervously. Mr. D had our attention now. For a moment, he stuttered and stammered on about something, I'm not sure what, and then he just pressed on with the class like a good soldier.

We didn't realize it at the time, but we had just witnessed what was probably the biggest public foul-up of our teacher's entire life.

The following week, we had a meeting with all of our parents. Mr. D didn't show up, but he passed along an apology for the kick. What else could he do? Our parents encouraged us to be more cooperative with our teachers, but we got the idea that Mr. D was in more trouble than we were.

I'm not sure Mr. D ever taught another Bible class after that. But maybe he did. After a long while. After the dust had settled.

In 12th grade, the College Church youth minister taught our Sunday morning Bible class. He was a nice enough guy. A little goofy acting, but nice, and he settled in on the topic of "Revelation." Each Sunday, he'd put up the same overhead graphic on our classroom wall, a picture of angels with swords on horses on clouds (or something like that), and then he'd talk about the upcoming end of the world.

I lasted only a few weeks in there. Because...

...Some guy in my class, some person who shall henceforth remain nameless, had the idea to skip Bible class and go out for breakfast at the local Hardees.

Decision time: The book of Revelation or Hardees?

Did I mention we were in 12th grade?

And so to Hardees we went. Every Sunday. There were about 4 of us regulars, and some others who would join in from time to time. Everyone was welcome. We'd meet up outside of the College Church annex building, hop into someone's car, and take off down Race Street for a large plastic plate's worth of biscuits and gravy and hash browns or some other fried morning favorite. We'd kick back and talk and relax and then head on back to church in time for the main worship service.

I loved those Sunday mornings.

By the next year, my freshman year in college, I was

mostly back on board with attending Sunday morning Bible class.

Mostly.

———

Cheryl (b. 1967)

Loretta Jones taught my 5th and 6th-grade Bible class.

Once a month, on a Sunday afternoon, Mrs. Jones would take three or four of us kids to visit the "old-folks home." At the nursing home, all of us would file into a room, where we'd sit on a flower-patterned couch and listen to Loretta being so kind to these older people. (She had already told us that we didn't have to say much, but that our job was "to bring the light of youth into the room.")

After our visitation time, Mrs. Jones would sometimes take us to Weiner King for hotdogs before the evening worship service.

Craig (b. 1969)

The boys in our church participated in a "Timothy Class," where we learned how to publicly read scriptures, lead singing and offer up prayers.

Songs of the Church

Typically, the Church of Christ does not use any musical instruments during a worship service. All of the songs are sung a cappella.

———

We used to sing some rowdy songs in Bible class. Songs like:

"Roll the Gospel Chariot Along."

And we'd furiously roll our arms in circles, like chariot wheels, squashing the devil like a bug into the ground.

"The Wise Man Built His House Upon the Rock."

And the rain came tumbling down. Oh, the rain came down, and the floods came up ... and the wise man's house stood firm.

The wise man did fine in his verse, but the foolish man wasn't so lucky. His house was built on the sand and went SPLAT when the rains came down. (I wonder if the foolish man was in the house when that happened?) We would always yell the SPLAT-part and clap our hands together loudly.

"One-Two-Three, the Devil's After Me."

The devil is chucking bricks (or sticks) at us, and fortunately, he's a bad shot. He never hits us! (I wish that were true.)

"I'm In Right Out Right Up Right Down."
Right happy all the time.

Lots of hand movements here and a song that increased in speed. A great cardio workout. We're "happy all the time." All the time? Hmmm.

"If You're Happy and You Know It."
Clap your hands.

But what should you do if you're not happy? Stick your hands in your pockets? What if you might be happy, but you just don't know it? Maybe this song asked more questions than it answered.

"Father Abraham."
Many sons had Father Abraham. I am one of them, and so are you, so let's all praise the Lord. Right arm! Left arm!

Rarely sung. Maybe because it led to occasional "accidental" punches for the person on my left and right.

I can picture myself sitting in a classroom on a Sunday morning. I'm surrounded by friends in a circle of tiny plastic chairs. Our middle-aged teacher with perfectly coiffed brown hair smiles as we sing these songs, but her eyes grow wide as we get a little too, well, rowdy. After that, we turn quickly to more subdued tunes like "Into My Heart" or "Tiptoe Tiptoe in God's House" or "The Lord Is in His Holy Temple." And from there, we move on to a chain prayer to calm things down even more.

Bible class could be a bit of a roller coaster. Noisy songs followed by restrained songs. But the rowdy songs were only for Bible class. They never made their way into the auditorium, into the church service proper.

———

"... as we stand together and sing."

Invitation song time.

My dad loved the invitation song. After 45 minutes of preaching his guts out, he was ready to see if some fruit would come walking down the aisles.

And he usually wasn't disappointed. He had a God-given ability to get people to the front of the auditorium for baptism or restoration.

"Jimmy, what would you like for an invitation song?" song leaders would often ask.

"Well, I always think 'Just As I Am' and 'Why Not Tonight' are about the most effective," he'd reply.

And he was right. A fiery sermon and 6 verses of "Just As I Am" usually did the trick.

Just as I am! with-out one plea,
But that Thy blood was shed for me,
And that Thou bidd'st me come to Thee,
O Lamb of God, I come! I come!

And while we all rose to sing, Dad would be standing up front, right in the middle of the action, ready with a smile and a handshake for anyone who decided to come forward.

If there were lots of responses, he'd be ecstatic, and I'd think, "Oh yeah, man, here we go." And if things were slow, he'd gently raise his hand to the song leader to signal a pause. Then he'd march back into the pulpit to implore some more. And the people on the fence, the ones holding on to the back of the pew in front of them so tightly that their knuckles were turning white, well, some of them would step out and make a decision for the Lord.

Dad might pause the song leader two or three times during the invitation, if he thought it would help. He could read the audience like a book. No one escaped his roving glance, unless there were about a thousand people in the audience. Then, maybe a few would fail to catch his eye. Maybe.

Oh, why not to-night?
Oh, why not to-night?
Wilt thou be saved?
Then why not to-night?

———

By the mid-1990s, my wife Cheryl and I had a baby son, Cal, who absolutely positively hated his car seat. HATED it. Just about any trip, be it five minutes or five hours, Cal would be screaming his lungs out from the backseat. Cheryl and I didn't know what to do or where to turn. It was a miserable existence. Until one day we found...

Jerome Williams, a cappella singer.

His soulful voice, pouring out of our Volkswagen cassette player, took the cry right out of Cal.

...You Are The Song That I Sing...
...I Want To Be Where You Are...
...God Is So Good...

When other families told us about their screaming babies, we'd always say, "You gotta try Jerome."

———

Steven (b. 1967)

I learned to lead singing as a kid and was regularly asked to lead the congregation on Sunday evenings.

Craig (b. 1969)

Our congregation added some "new" songs to our *Great Songs of the Church* songbooks. The additional pages, which included "The New Song" and "Salvation Has Been Brought Down," were glued into the front and back of our books.

Elisabeth (b. 193X)

The best thing about the church in Searcy was the singing. At Sheridan, we had such a small group, and the singing was pitiful. When I heard the singing at College Church, I was in heaven.

Preaching the Word

Preaching was a big deal. A church could grow or decline quickly based on the quality of its weekly preaching. Also, once or twice a year, a local congregation could be energized by having a dynamic speaker brought in for a gospel meeting.

The College Church always had a stable of talented preachers, from teachers at Harding to the ministry staff who regularly filled the pulpit on Sundays.

———

Dad was gone a lot.

Driving. Flying. Driving some more.

Checking in and out of motels.

Shaking hands. Patting folks on back.

Preaching the gospel. Teaching Bible classes.

Restoring the weak. Baptizing the lost. Imploring more people to come forward during the invitation.

Conducting Friday-to-Sunday meetings, Sunday-to-Wednesday meetings, Sunday-to-Friday meetings, or Sunday-to-Sunday-to Wednesday meetings.

And then, at the end of it all...

He would come back home. Road weary. Rumpled button-down white shirt and loosened tie. Briefcase in one hand and suitcase in the other. Ready for a cold Dr. Pepper and nice home-cooked meal.

———

Since Dad spoke at so many different churches, he could get away with telling the same jokes over and over again.

A few of his favorites:

A man walks up to Dad in the church lobby, shakes his hand and says, "How are you doing, Brother Allen?" Dad grins back saying, "Well, I never felt better when I had less."

Dad is preaching and makes an especially solid point. Someone from the audience shouts, "Amen!" Dad smiles and says, "You know what an 'amen' does for a preacher? Well, it's like saying sic 'em to a bulldog."

After a potluck meal at the church building, Dad begins his sermon by saying something like, "Brethren, you all sure know how to put on a good spread around here. I know one thing for certain…"—he pauses and rubs his tummy for effect—"…I will not be speaking about the sin of gluttony tonight."

———

Dad described the afterlife as "an eternity in heaven" for people who were saved or "an eternity in hell" for people who were lost. Then, he would sometimes share an example like this:

An ant walks around a metal ball the size of the earth. He walks along the equator, day after day, week after week, month after month, year after year. Just walking and walking and walking. Well, by the time that ant has worn a path an inch deep or a foot deep or even all the way to the core of this earth-sized metal ball, then eternity would have only just begun.

For the life of me, I still can't get the image of that marching ant out of my head.

———

Evening gospel meeting with us school-aged kids sitting up front.

Fiery sermon and a long invitation song.

People, young and old, come streaming down the aisles.

A few of them, mostly women and girls, are crying.

The young want to be baptized; the old want to be restored.

So many are coming forward that there aren't enough seats for everyone.

Which brings me to the best part.

The elders, the ones receiving the responders, pause. They give us kids—all of us singing our lungs out—a little nod.

We vacate our seats and go to stand in front of the stage.

We look out at the crowd, at the responders who just keep coming. We stand there, grinning like fools.

We're a part of this mass of moving people. We're giving up our seats, so more can come forward.

We're watching the world change right before our very eyes.

———

Craig (b. 1955)

When I heard Jim Woodroof preach at the College church, I thought, "I've never heard preaching like that! What do you mean it's all about Jesus and not about being right on all the issues?!"

Jimmy (b. 1960)

Landon Saunders talked about "The Father's Business." He shared how the business of the Father must be our business and how the "busyness" of the Father must be our "busyness." He said that if our business was not the Father's business, then we were not using our lives as God intended.

Elisabeth (b. 193X)

In the fall of 1942, Daddy found out about a young man who had just finished at Harding and who was working for the defense plant at Pine Bluff. His name was Jim Bill McInteer, and he came to preach for us two Sundays a month for about four years. His preaching made such a difference in our tiny congregation. (We had 8 to 10 people and only one other young person besides my brother and me.) Jim Bill gave good lessons, and he showed us that you could have fun and enjoy life and still be a good Christian. He was a big influence in my choosing to attend Harding College.

Cheryl (b. 1967)

During my high school years, Kristy Thomas led the women's prison ministry at our church. We went to the jail week after week, and I saw the Holy Spirit at work in the life of Kristy and in the lives of the women she was teaching.

Kristy died 10 years ago on my birthday. I'm sure Jesus was glad to finally meet this woman who'd told so many other people about Him.

Baptism

Baptism was the biggest thing that happened at church. It was a time when the believer's sins were considered forgiven. Baptism was a complete immersion in water, not a sprinkling or pouring of water on a person's head. Generally an individual had to be at least 8 years old or so—old enough to know what he or she was doing—to be considered ready for baptism.

In order to be baptized, a person had to have faith in Jesus and an understanding of repentance (a turning from sin). After the event, some churches would place an asterisk (*) by the individual's name in the church directory to show that baptism had taken place.

———

I was baptized on August 31, 1976, a month after the United States Bicentennial celebration. If you'd asked me my age, I would have told you, "Ten and a half."

A few weeks before, I'd discussed my decision with a friend. We were standing by the creek which ran behind the Harding College football field.

"I'm thinking of getting baptized soon," I said.

"Okay," he replied. (He'd already been baptized.)

In the fall and spring school semesters, the College

Church held a gospel meeting which ran from Sunday through Friday. In 1976, the fall meeting kicked off on August 29. It took me a couple of days to work up my nerve.

On Tuesday night, I sat on the front row beside a couple of friends. After an hour or so, we rose to sing the invitation song. I stood, but hesitated. It felt so comfortable just staying there. My heart was pounding in my chest. I stared at the man closest to me who was accepting responses. It felt kind of awkward, but I finally willed myself forward and shook the man's hand. He guided me right back to my seat. My friends sat down beside me to show their support.

Next came a very small clipboard with a pencil and invitation card. I could check a box for "baptism" or for "prayer." I checked the appropriate box and paused before writing, "I want to be baptized by my dad." I had trouble remembering if "baptize" was spelled with an "s" or a "z." I think I got it right. The man at the front smiled as he looked over my card.

During the public reading of all the response cards, Dad made his way down to the front. We walked together through the auditorium's front door and up the left staircase. (The right-side staircase was for girls who were getting baptized.) My friends followed us up to the changing room.

A few moments later, I slipped on the white baptismal garments and trailed my dad down some steps into the

baptistery.   Someone above us flipped a switch to part
the curtains, opening things up for the audience to see. I
felt a thousand pairs of eyes on me. Dad leaned forward
and talked into the baptistery microphone, saying, "I now
baptize you in the name of the Father. And of the Son. And
of the Holy Spirit."

The next thing I knew, I was getting pushed under the
water. I was so excited. I could feel those sins getting
washed away.

———

Shortly after my baptism...

Praying in my top-bunk bed.

Resting in the yellow glow of a lamp propped up on my
headboard.

Feeling the presence of God.

Wrapped up in His warm embrace.

Loved by Him and secure.

———

Mrs. Pryor, the wife of a Harding Bible professor, had
the first vanity license plate I ever saw. It said TREVA on
the back of her car.

After seeing it, I thought long and hard about a vanity
plate for our family. I finally settled on ACTS 238.

"Then Peter said unto them, Repent, and be baptized every one of you in the name of Jesus Christ for the remission of sins, and ye shall receive the gift of the Holy Ghost." Acts 2:38.

We never got a personalized tag, but I do believe Dad would have enjoyed cruising around town with that verse on the back of his truck.

————

Mary (b. 195X)

Sometimes preachers would encourage people to be baptized, saying, "The clothes are prepared, the water is warm, come while we stand together and sing."

Donald (b. 195X)

I got baptized after hearing a sermon titled "What Is Hell Like?" I felt like I was sprinting down the aisle during that invitation song. I was 9 years old, and I did NOT want to go to hell!

Wesley (b. 1968)

I was re-baptized, and I'm still not sure it took.

COLLEGE CHURCH of CHRIST

Area Code 501/268-7156   •   *712 East Race Avenue*   •   *Searcy, Arkansas 72143*

September 8, 1976

Dear Mike,

Congratulations on your becoming a Christian. Welcome
to the family!

Now that you have been born of the water and the Spirit,
you will want to develop a strong faith in Him. This
will be your shield against the daily pressures of life.
May I suggest that you set aside a time every day for
Bible reading and prayer. A booklet is enclosed that
will be helpful in your Bible study. Now, "as a newborn
babe, long for the sincere milk of the word that you may
grow thereby to salvation".

Any way the elders, Terry Smith or I can be of service
to you, please feel free to call on us. May God bless
you richly.

With kind regards,

FOR THE ELDERS

Jim Woodroof
Minister

dj
Encl: 1

Potlucking in the Fellowship Hall

"Potluck" meals were a big social event at church. Members could contribute to the feast by bringing in a main dish, a side dish, a salad, a dessert, soft drinks, paper plates, napkins, plastic cutlery, plastic cups, or some combination of the above.

Typically, the men of the church would set up tables and chairs while the women would get everything ready to set out buffet-style.

———

Cheryl and I attended several churches that had regular potlucks. It wasn't uncommon to see spaghetti with meatballs, Mexican casserole, and fried chicken presented on the same food table. I usually played it safe, going for the dishes my wife had prepared and potato chips.

You could never go wrong with potato chips.

———

Mary (b. 195X)

We had "watermelon feeds," "dinners on the grounds," and "ice cream suppers." We didn't express our emotions in words, but we'd try to feed the sadness right out of a person!

Steven (b. 1967)

Our church would sometimes have a game night and potluck meal at someone's home.

After about five desserts, I would start to feel a little sick.

VBS

Vacation Bible School, a weeklong Sunday-school program, took place every summer at the church building. Sometimes several Churches of Christ would work together to host a VBS. One motive behind the program was to pull in kids (and their families) who would not otherwise come out to church.

―――――

I attended VBS all over town. Downtown Church. Westside Church. And, of course, the College Church.

There we sang songs that were especially reserved for VBS.

Booster, booster, be a booster;
Don't be grouchy like a rooster;
Booster, booster, be a booster;
And boost our Bible school.
Boost!

And we also sang:

The B-I-B-L-E;
Yes, that's the book for me;

I stand alone on the Word of God;
The B-I-B-L-E!

(I think every VBS song ended with an exclamation mark!)

————

One year at Westside church, the teachers gave us Smile-Have-a-Nice-Day nametags. Our teacher, a very nice and chuckley woman, would joke around with us saying, "Why look at Jack, he's wearing two smiles today." Meaning, Jack had a yellow-smiley-face nametag, and he also had a smile on his face. Ha, ha, ha. We really did think that was funny.

Later in the week, I decided to wear my yellow-smiley-face sweatshirt to church. (Yes, I knew I'd get sweaty, but thought the sacrifice was worth it.) When I arrived at Bible class, the teacher exclaimed, "Why look at Mike, he's wearing 3 smiles today!"

I was pumped about VBS.

————

Downtown church was cool, because at the end of the morning they would roll out cases of Orange and Grape Crush soda. What a treat! Some of the boys would put their thumbs over the ends of the bottles and shake them up and then spray everyone around. Not me. I sucked down every drop. Drinking Grape Crush was like drinking liquid gold. We never had it at home.

———

As we got older, sometimes morning baseball practices would conflict with VBS, so our moms would pick us up at the church building and take us to practice or take us to practice and then drop us off at the church building. Either way, there were lots of pairs of dirty cleats tramping up and down those linoleum hallways.

———

Regina (b. 1968)

At VBS, we loved eating ice cream out of cups with flat wooden "spoons."

At Camp

Church Camp

The Church of Christ sponsors summer Christian camps across the country.

I attended Camp Takodah near Floral, Arkansas during my late elementary school years. It was there I first began taking notice of the opposite sex.

———

Ha – la – la – la...

I cringe. Oh, no. Please dear God, not that song.

Jesus is a friend next to ya...

I mean, it has a nice tune and is kind of catchy, and it's not too terrible if you're scrunched in between a bunch of boys. BUT, if you are sitting next to a girl or even close to a girl, then you are in big trouble.

Ha – la – la – la...

Here it comes. We're all standing up now. Singing. Shouting. Laughing. Boys are on one side of the outdoor gym. Girls are on the other side. Me, I'm standing on the edge of the boys' side and about six feet away from a girl who's just about my age.

Take the hand next to ya...

That verse lasted for—ev—er. Okay, this girl is a little bit cute and my palms are sweating like crazy. Did she just wipe her hand on the side of her jeans?

Ha – la – la – la...

Okay, be cool. I'll lean on my right leg with my hands on my hips. This is no big deal. I can do this.

Give a hug next to ya...

Yikes almighty! That was awful. A quick side hug and a pat on the back. She didn't seem to mind it, though. She's even giggling. GIGGLING. I'm in agony over here, and she thinks this is so funny?! What is this counselor-song leading-guy trying to do to us? Torture us? Punish us for not properly cleaning our cabins? It's not right! Let me go on the record to say that holding hands and hugging during a devotional IS NOT GOOD. Would Jesus approve of all this?

Ha – la – la – la...

Thank goodness! We made it. Now let's all sit down and catch our breath. How about a nice slow song, Mr. Counselor?

Jesus is Lord,
My redeemer.
How he loves me,
How I love him...

Ahh. Good choice, sir. Very good choice.

I look over at the girl. She glances back at me and quickly looks away.

————

I met Harvey at Camp Takodah when we were both 11-years-old. He was a funny, absentminded kid with sun-bleached hair. The boys in our cabin started calling him "Harvey Squirrel," except we would say it like this, "Harvey Squaw-Earlllll!" We thought this was hilarious. Surprisingly, Harvey turned out to be a bit of a ladies' man and landed himself a 14-year-old girlfriend named Lorie. We were all amazed.

During the second week of camp, the staff organized a "Sadie Hawkins Night." It was a tortuous event that began on the baseball diamond. Clumps of sweaty boys stood in the outfield grass. The girls gathered around the dirt infield. When the whistle blew, each girl zeroed in on a boy and gave chase. If she was quick enough and tagged him, then the couple would be "married" by the camp director and spend the rest of the evening together.

On that terrible night, the whistle blew. Harvey was a bit slow of foot and got picked off by a girl not named Lorie. I didn't get tagged, or even chased much for that matter. After awhile, there were about four of us boys left in the outfield. That's when Lorie came flying around third base and knocked me over. She seemed peeved that someone else had gotten to her beloved Harvey first. I got up, dusted myself off, and headed over to the outdoor gymnasium with my new sweetheart.

At the gym, Lorie and I waited in line for Coach Ed to perform our "wedding ceremony." When we finally made it to the makeshift altar, Coach Ed grinned and pronounced us "husband and wife." Harvey joined us a few minutes later for some hot dogs and baked beans. Evidently, he'd gotten a quickie divorce from his Sadie wife. The three of us ate by the hopscotch court and remained together for a volleyball game. By the 9 o'clock devotional, Harvey was holding hands with my better half.

I walked back to my cabin that night alone. I was glad to have been picked for Sadie Hawkins, but felt a little sad that I'd been someone's second choice.

———

David (b. 1966)

I often thought Christianity was kind of boring, but camp helped change my mind.

Regina (b. 1968)

I went to Camp Ne-O-Tez in DeSoto, Missouri. It rained all week.

On one clear night, though, the camp counselors decided to build us a campfire. We all hiked up a hill to see the big fire, and when we got to the top, it started raining like crazy. We had to form a "human chain" in order to make it safely back to our cabins.

Steven (b. 1967)

My college roommate was my best friend from camp.

Rachelle (b.1965)

One night we were singing "Kumbaya" around the camp fire.

"Someone's crying Lord, kumbaya."

"Someone's singing Lord, kumbaya."

We sang so many verses; I thought it was never going to end.

Finally, a guy named George led a final verse, "Someone's flossing Lord, kumbaya. Someone's flossing Lord, kumbaya." Everyone sang along, and then we all died laughing.

At School

Harding Academy

Harding Academy is a Church of Christ-associated elementary and secondary school located a few blocks from my childhood home in Searcy. (By the way, there is another Church of Christ school called Harding Academy which is in Memphis, Tennessee.) I attended "The Academy" from 1st grade through 12th grade.

————

Our 3rd grade teacher, Mrs. Lawson, announced to our class that we would be memorizing First Corinthians 13, the chapter on love. It seemed daunting. A whole chapter? All of those verses sticking in our brains and then coming out of our mouths?

She opened up her big black Bible to the book of First Corinthians. She said, "Now, boys and girls, I want you to know that I am a very clean person. I wash my hands every day. But look at this page in my Bible." She held it up for everyone to see. "I have read from First Corinthians 13 so many times that the oils from my hands have turned the page yellow."

She was right. The double-columned page with tiny black print was dingy and yellow. It was kind of cool and gross all at the same time.

And so we began to memorize the chapter, a verse or so each day. Mrs. Lawson would read a phrase from her King James Version Bible (always substituting the word "love" for the KJV word "charity"), and we would repeat it back to her as a class.

"Rejoiceth not in iniquity," she would read.

"Rejoiceth not in iniquity," we would respond.

After we had learned all the verses, we quoted it as a group for the rest of the elementary school at a Friday assembly. I don't think anyone clapped afterward, but they should have. It was a sight to behold.

Though I speak with the tongues of men and of angels, and have not love, I am become as sounding brass, or a tinkling cymbal.

I still remember most of it today.

Thank you, Mrs. Lawson.

———

In elementary school, we prayed in our classrooms. I often tended to talk to God about things I was worried about, like the spread of communism.

At some point, I'd seen a film that showed communism spilling like blood from Russia onto other countries on a giant map. After awhile, the whole world started looking very red. Also, at about the same time, Dad mentioned to me that Searcy would be one of the first places attacked in a nuclear war because of missile silos located near our town. HOLY COW! Why did they put missiles around Searcy? Weren't there some deserts or someplace else out West where they could put them? I did not want bombs to fall on Arkansas! I did not want the communists to take over America! So I prayed:

Dear Father in Heaven,

Thank you for this day and for all the many blessings of it.

Thank you for our food and for everything you've given us.

Thank you for our families and for our friends.

Thank you for letting us live in this free country, and please help us to be safe from communism.

It's in Jesus name I pray,

Amen.

————

One year, we all prayed like crazy for David.

David was a tall, athletic high-school guy and the son of a Harding College vice-president. In elementary school, we looked up to David and other senior high football players who sported red and black Harding Academy letter jackets. They were like rock stars to us.

One night during football season, David got into a pretty serious car accident, and he broke his neck or his back and maybe some other stuff. Everyone was concerned. We all came to school sharing the news we'd heard from our parents.

"David is doing better."

"He's going to be out of the hospital soon."

"One of the doctors, a man who doesn't even go to church, said that he doesn't know how David would have survived the crash without God's help."

And so we prayed. Every day. And pretty soon, David got well.

———

Our 6th grade teacher, Mrs. Alexander, challenged us to read the Bible. If we read the New Testament, or if we read the entire Bible during the school year, then we'd get a certificate at the 6th grade graduation ceremony.

"Forget this New-Testament-only stuff," I thought, "I'm reading the whole thing."

And so I began on page one of the Old Testament, gobbling up Genesis, tearing through Exodus, and then finding myself lost in the trackless desert of Leviticus.

"Who wants to read this junk? Rules about mildew? MILDEW? Why didn't Mrs. Alexander warn us about the third book of Moses?"

I lost my momentum and fell about 20 chapters behind schedule. I realized there would be no certificate waiting for me on graduation day.

Doggone Leviticus!

———

One time in high school chapel, a teacher was reading the announcements and said something funny. I mean really funny. We all died laughing.

As the noise died down, the teacher looked out at the audience and said, "Okay, let's wipe the smiles off our faces; it's time to read the Bible."

———

On another morning, we had an "air band" concert during chapel. In the same auditorium where we had a once-a-week hymn sing, a bunch of upperclassmen put on tight jeans and pretended to play guitars and drums. They lip-synched "I Love Rock and Roll" and "Our Lips Are Sealed." It was awesome. I still can't believe they talked a teacher into letting them do it.

One student in the audience was so upset by the concert that she got up and left chapel in protest. The rest of us stayed and rocked on. For one day anyway.

———

Jeff and I took the same high school Bible class at Harding Academy, and we had a big assignment coming up. We were supposed to write a two-page paper on a spiritual topic of our own choosing. I decided early on to draw some inspiration from a favorite scripture or devotional book. As the deadline drew nearer, though, my plan began to change.

> WARNING: What I'm about to tell you is a wrong thing to do. If you are asked to write a Bible class paper, please do not take the following course of action.

Okay, back to the story. The night before our papers were due, Jeff came over to my house. Neither one of us had written a word.

I said, "Hey, Jeff, why don't we just copy a chapter out of this here book, *Nuggets of Gold* by Donald E. Wildmon?"

Jeff said, "Sounds good."

I said, "I'll take chapter 13, 'An Open Letter to the Graduate' based on Proverbs 1:7. You take chapter 14, 'A

Tribute to the Elderly' based on Psalm 71:9."

Jeff said, "Sounds good."

And that's what we did. We copied the chapters word-for-word. I take that back; we may have changed a couple of words. And the next day, Jeff and I turned in our papers.

When we got them back a few days later, I had made a 100. Jeff scored a 95.

I know; I know. In hindsight, I probably should have given Jeff chapter 13.

———

Fearon was a year older than me and president of the student body at Harding Academy. He was a likeable guy with a big smile and brown hair that swooped off to one side. He sort of looked like a member of the band Devo.

During my junior year, the College Church youth minister asked Fearon and me to speak at a Wednesday night worship service. Fearon seemed very cool and confident about the whole thing, as if speaking in front of a thousand people was no big deal. Me, on the other hand? Well, I felt a little nauseous.

The big Wednesday night finally arrived, and Fearon was awesome. Completely. He preached about being surrendered to God. He talked about having this junky old car that really didn't belong to him, because it belonged to

God. Fearon said if he got himself into an accident, then hey, that was okay, because the car was God's car. God could do whatever He wanted to do with His car. Right?

Fearon was mesmerizing. In that 5-minute sermon, he had IT. Charm? Charisma? The Holy Spirit? I'm not sure what IT was, but IT was there.

I'll be honest. I was a little jealous.

————

We had a minor league baseball player come and speak in chapel one day. He was a clean-cut, articulate guy who seemed like an action hero from a comic book. He told us about playing baseball and about being married to a beauty pageant queen (a former Miss Georgia or something). He also shared about his faith and about how important it was for us to follow God's commands and the laws of our country. As an example, he mentioned having a strong conviction about obeying the posted speed limits.

He said, "I hate driving the speed limit. I hate driving that slow. Cars pass me all the time, and it gives me a headache. But I know it's what God wants me to do, so I drive 55 on the highway."

Even though I was old enough to drive and pretty regularly exceeded the speed limit (having once actually reached 85 mph on a trip to Kansas), I was impressed with this baseball player's sincerity. He was putting his faith into action.

I still think about the baseball player sometimes when I'm riding in my car. I wonder if he continues to observe the speed limit. I wonder if he's the guy I just passed on I-40.

———

My friend Kim, a quiet guy who smiled a lot, died during our junior year. Dad broke the news to me on a Sunday morning before church.

Kim and I had played baseball on the same Buddy League team. He was shortstop. I was first base.

In 4th grade, we met for Cub Scouts at his house. He had a CB radio in his garage.

About a week before he died, Kim and I had split a pizza at Mazzio's restaurant. Everything seemed okay.

At the funeral, I didn't really feel close to God or even comforted. I mostly felt sad and numb.

———

Rachelle (b. 1965)

One of the girls in my high school Bible class was so serious. She would cry sometimes about all of the lost souls in the world.

Harding University

Harding University (a.k.a. Harding College prior to 1979) is a Church of Christ-associated school located just down the road from Harding Academy in Searcy. I attended "The University" from 1984 to 1989, majoring in journalism and physical education.

————

My next door neighbor on Magnolia Drive was 3 years older than me and attended the University of Arkansas in Fayetteville. I thought, I could go live with Roy and get the whole public college experience. I talked to Dad about it one night while we were standing in the hallway by my room.

He listened to my spiel and said, "Let me put it to you this way. You can go to Harding, and I'll pay for it, or you can go somewhere else and pay for it yourself. It's your decision."

I decided to go to Harding.

————

Dad was the guest speaker at the College Church on my first Sunday as an undergraduate. The auditorium was packed with returning students. Dad's lesson that morning focused on what parents should expect from their children at Harding.

The CliffsNotes version: "Hey, kids, don't be wild!"

I sat on a pew in the balcony and thought the lesson was a little strange. You see, Dad had never talked to me about these things before. He seemed more comfortable giving advice to a big audience than he would have been in sharing it just with me.

————

I felt frustrated in college. So many rules! Oh my goodness! Curfew (11pm on weekdays, midnight on the weekends). Dress code (no shorts in the classroom). Grooming code (short hair, no beards). Mandatory chapel attendance (only 10 skips allowed per semester). Yikes! It could feel suffocating at times.

But Harding was a safe place. I understand that now. I felt safe and protected there.

————

Walking across campus early in the morning. Early for me. Must be before 8 o'clock.

Heading north on a sidewalk between the old softball field and the backside of the library. It's a little overcast and chilly – sweatshirt weather.

There's a guy in front of me. He's tall and skinny and takes each step in a bouncing stride. Something about the way he moves reminds me of a pole vaulter taking off down the runway. I've seen him around, and I'm pretty sure he's a Bible major, but I wouldn't swear to it.

We continue on the path toward the cafeteria. His long, energetic strides carry him further away from me.

All of a sudden, the guy raises both hands high over his head. He shouts at the top of his lungs, "This is the day which the LORD hath made! We will rejoice and be glad in it!"

I slow my pace just a bit more. "Weird," I think.

————

I ran for Harding student body president in the spring of 1987. I don't know why I ran. Okay, that's not exactly true. I had a couple of underlying motives.

Reason #1: Get a nice résumé bullet.

Reason #2: Impress my dad. (He was Harding student body president way back in 1950-something.)

I was prepared. I understood the basics of campaigning:

Strategy #1: Put up attractive and correctly-spelled posters throughout the student center. (Thank you future-wife Cheryl.)

Strategy #2: Walk around campus talking to a bunch of

people, especially freshman. (The freshman vote is important, because they actually vote.)

Strategy #3: Give a good "elect-me" speech in chapel.

The first 2 seemed easy, so I spent the bulk of my time preparing for number 3. I practiced my speech all the time. In my dorm room. In the shower. While driving. I learned to hate that speech.

On chapel presentation day, the three presidential candidates--Joel, Ragan, and me--sat on the stage in our sharpest duds. We were ready to go.

Joel was a tall cool drink of water. He looked like a president. Heck, he looked The President of the United States. Ragan, on the other hand, wasn't quite so intimidating to me. He seemed more like the kid next door, the one you'd play wiffleball with.

And so we took our turns. And when Ragan stood up behind the podium, he gave this sort of deep and spiritually-focused speech. "Wow," I thought, "This guy should be president. Why, if I wasn't voting for myself, I'd definitely be voting for him."

Next to Ragan, my speech felt like, "Blah, Blah, Blah, Blah, Blah. Let's have some fun next year, okay? Blah, Blah."

On voting day, all of us candidates hung around the student association office awaiting the results.

The announcement came. Ragan had finished third.

Joel and I moved on to a runoff election, which I eventually won.

It seemed kind of ironic to me.

As a student at Harding, I got to speak in chapel a few times. If I had another shot, I'd probably crack a couple of lame jokes and then say something like this:

"If you've already had sex. If you drink alcohol or do drugs sometimes. If you cheat or lie or steal. If you eat too much or worry too much or feel lonely or suicidal. In any of these circumstances or in any other situation that you could possibly imagine, there is this incredible God who loves you no matter what. As a Christian, you are his beautiful son or daughter, and He could not be more proud of you."

I might say something like that.

Sometimes I wonder what my life would have been like if I hadn't gone to Harding.

I think, oh man, I could have joined the military right out of high school. I could have been a freaking Navy seal, killing commies all over the planet. Hoo Yah!

Or maybe …

I could have studied archeology at Memphis State University. Ancient history was always my big interest, especially after seeing the Indiana Jones movies. Yeah, I could have discovered the tomb of some old African king that no one had ever heard of before. That would have been kind of exhilarating, right?

Then again …

How about a cop? I could have been a police detective. Breaking down doors and bringing young punks to justice. I would have liked that (as long as the punks were mostly mild-mannered).

But in the end, I always come back to this point. Any way these daydreams play out, I have a major problem. If I didn't attend Harding, then I wouldn't have met Cheryl, the love of my life. Yeah, I would have missed out on that.

Okay, now that I think about it, maybe the Harding scenario wasn't such a bad one after all.

———

Craig (b. 1969)

When I was in kindergarten, my dad decided to leave the coaching profession and attend preaching school at Harding College. Back then it was known as the Christian Communications Program. For Dad's first year in the program, our family stayed in Benton while dad would spend the week in Searcy staying with his mom.

That was a tough year for me (and my mom, brother and sister). We only saw Dad on the weekends.

Kevin (b. 1966)

We had to go to chapel every day, and I noticed that most people (including myself) weren't tuned in to anything that happened in there.

Life and Doctrine

Preachers' and Elders' Kids

All of my life, my dad has been a traveling preacher. He's held gospel meetings all over the place. He's helped many people come to know the Lord. He's done a lot of good.

————

Dad had a tough childhood.

His mother died in a car accident when he was 11. His father was never around. He and his grandmother were homeless for a time.

In many ways, I had an easier beginning. For the first 18 years of my life, I never remember having to introduce myself in a church or school situation. Everyone already knew me.

"That's Mike Allen. He's Jimmy's boy."

————

In elementary school, one of my teachers wrote a poem for our class. Here's what she wrote about me:

Michael Allen loves the Bible
He's glad his dad's a preacher,

He does his lessons very well
And watches sports from the bleachers.

————

Over the years, whenever I talked about what I wanted to do when I grew up, Dad would chime in and say, "You should be a preacher."

That was it. Just, you should be a preacher.

End of discussion.

————

I've had a bunch, and I mean a bunch, of conversations in my life that went something like this:

ENTHUSIASTIC OLDER GUY: (faraway look in his eyes) Why I remember when your daddy preached at the Jackson Street Church of Christ way back in 1964. It was wonderful. My little brother was baptized during that meeting.

ME: (forced smile) That's great.

E.O.G.: How's your dad doing these days?

ME: He's doing fine.

E.O.G.: Is he still holding meetings?

ME: He is. He's slowed down some lately, but he's still out there preaching.

E.O.G.: That's good. What an amazing man. Does he still fish?

ME: Oh yeah. He still loves to fish.

E.O.G.: Alright. I sure would love to see him again sometime. (pause) Well, the next time you talk to your dad, be sure to tell him George Smith from Monroe, Louisiana was asking about him.

ME: I sure will.

I've gotta tell you, these conversations used to annoy the daylights out of me. That may be putting it mildly. These guys (or occasionally gals) only wanted to talk about my father, sometimes for as long as 10 or 15 minutes.

But nowadays, these conversations aren't happening so much. And on those rare occasions when they do, I don't seem to mind. I tend to think, "Wow, my dad gave this guy something. Some encouragement. Some hope. At the very least, a really good moment in his life."

————

In the summer of 2004, Cheryl, our kids, and I moved from Connecticut to Northern Virginia so that I could start a new job. We hardly knew anyone in the area. It was a lonely and difficult time.

One afternoon, I had a chance to bend the ear of a confidante. I said, "Rob, who am I if people around here don't know me as Jimmy Allen's son?"

Without hesitation, he replied, "Mike, you're God's son. That's what matters."

———

Cindy (b. 1959)

I was grateful for the fact that my father was not as "narrow" as other preachers and church members were at that time. I was blessed to be taught the concept of grace, a broader view of divorce and remarriage, and a biblical view of race. I believe these positive experiences were why I decided God was calling me to be a preacher's wife.

Regina (b. 1968)

My dad became an elder when I was about 14. It put pressure on me to try to look and act perfectly.

Mission Trips

Missions were a big deal.

Students traveled during Spring Break or over the summer to help churches all around the globe.

Doctors and nurses took medical mission trips.

Other people dedicated a good portion of their lives to working on the mission field. These missionaries were often held in high esteem. Even after they had returned to the States, it wasn't unusual to hear them introduced at church as "having served for many years as a missionary to…"

Harding University sponsored "International Campaigns," organizing groups of students to go oversees during the summer. I traveled to Australia in 1985 and to Italy in 1988. While there, our groups invited people to church, passed out Christian literature, and sang hymns in public squares.

Some students sweated bullets to collect funds for campaigns, but I had no trouble raising the dough because Dad knew so many people. We'd send off letters and the checks would start rolling in.

During my senior year in college, we raised $1,000 over the amount I needed to go to Italy.

———

Tom.

Harding Bible faculty member and campaign leader to The Land Down Under.

Not Dr. Eddins. Not Professor Eddins. Not Mr. Eddins. Not Brother Eddins.

"Just call me Tom," he said.

———

On a campaign to Italy, my friend Randy and I stayed with a Christian couple in Cervignano. She sold ice cream – *gelato*. Her husband was a cop.

I only knew a few words in Italian. For example, I knew "*caldo*" was hot and "*freddo*" was cold. I used these words as frequently as I could. I'd walk into the kitchen in the morning. "Brrrr. It's very *freddo*." The woman would smile. Later, I'd take a sip of coffee. "Ahhh. *Caldo*." And she would laugh.

One day, the woman told us the story of how she came to know Christ.

She said, "You see, boys, a few years ago I was out walking and saw a tiny booklet on the ground. I picked it up and read about a Bible course being offered for free! I filled out the information and took the course. I answered all of the questions. Afterward, I was baptized and became a member of the church here in Cervignano. What do you think of that?"

What do I think of that? Well, I think it's one of the sweetest stories I've ever heard.

———

Sitting on a bus.

Sitting on a bus in Italy (or maybe it's Spain) with my two friends Scott and Gregg.

We have just finished our senior year of college. We have just finished several weeks of an international campaign.

We are bored, and we begin to sing old high school chorus songs. The Italians (or possibly they are Spaniards) don't seem to mind. Maybe they are bored too.

And so we sing, the three of us together, as one slightly-off-key baritone and two deep-throated basses:

For all the saints, who from their labors rest,
who thee by faith before the world confessed,
thy name, O Jesus, be forever blest.
Alleluia, Alleluia!

I recently discovered a version of "For All the Saints" sung by Dan Haseltine of the Christian group Jars of Clay. He does a very nice job. But, dare I say, not quite as nice as three young men on the back of a bus in Italy (or Spain).

———

In 1998, we had a missionary family from Africa come to visit our family in Hawaii. On the first day, everyone was relaxing around the house when the missionary dad spotted a snake on our back porch. He leapt to his feet and said, "Don't move. Everyone be perfectly still."

Our 5-year-old daughter, Kate, looked at the missionary and then over at the serpent. It remained motionless, poised as if to strike. She then walked calmly out onto the porch and picked up the snake by its tail. She was not one bit afraid of the toy cobra she held in her hand.

We all thought this story was hilarious. If there was a lull in the conversation for the rest of the week, we could always mention the snake incident.

At the end of our time together, the missionary couple took Cheryl and me out for dinner. We had a nice meal and good conversation. And at one point, the missionary man paused to give us a little speech. "Uh oh," I thought, "What's this going to be?"

He said, "Mike and Cheryl, we just wanted you to know

that you're doing a great job here. You're hanging in there with God and with the church. You're helping other people. You're good parents who care about your kids. We just wanted to tell you that."

I felt a little embarrassed and at a loss for words. But I got it. He was giving us exactly what we needed at that time – a blessing.

———

Kim (b. 1979)

I was 14 when I went on my first mission trip to Honduras. While there, I saw the lives of people who were very different from me, but I came to realize that we shared the strongest possible bond – Christ!

Craig (b. 1969)

When I was 7-years-old, my family moved to Watertown, South Dakota as part of a 3-family mission team. There was a small congregation already there that had about 15-20 members.

Pretty soon, we began a bus ministry and hosted a special "Children's Bible Hour" service on Sunday afternoons. My job with the new ministry was to be the bus "runner." This meant I was the one who would jog up to a house, knock on the door, and tell our riders that the bus was there to pick them up. I also helped the smaller kids cross the street and get onto the bus.

Lectureships and Seminars

Church of Christ members loved getting together for conferences to learn about faith-related topics and issues. The events were usually hosted in church auditoriums, on Christian college campuses, or at larger convention venues.

————

When I was in junior high, my friend Brett asked me to help out at a seminar being held on the Harding University campus. His mom was co-sponsoring an event which addressed the dangers of "humanism." I wasn't sure I'd ever heard the word humanism before, but I sensed that it was something very bad.

I got up early on the Saturday morning of the seminar and put on some slacks and a nice shirt. There were four of us boys who were working as ushers for the day. Our first job was to welcome people at the door and point them to the registration tables inside the Benson Auditorium lobby. (We noted early on that the Benson, with its thousands of theater seats, was plenty big enough for the anti-humanism crowd.)

During the day, we ran a few errands, ate a free lunch, and got to listen to some of the lectures. I learned a lot about humanism, a godless way of thinking that could be found everywhere in our modern culture and which should be avoided at all costs. I guessed it was kind of like communism, maybe even worse. (Were all the "isms" bad?)

In the afternoon, a couple of us wandered up to the balcony. There were only a handful of people scattered among the seats up there.

I turned a corner and stopped in my tracks. "Wait a minute," I thought, "I know that guy! It's Dave Woodman, Channel 4 sportscaster and Voice of the Arkansas Razorbacks!"

How cool was that? Dave Woodman was on our side. He was against humanism too!

———

I had been dating Cheryl for a few months when the Brecheen/Faulkner Marriage Enrichment Seminar rolled into town. Beforehand, the seminar had been announced as an event for married couples or for couples who were considering tying the knot.

Cheryl and I decided to sign up.

We had heard about the seminar for years. (It was somewhat famous in Church of Christ circles.) And I thought, by attending early-on, we might be able to get ourselves out of some future pre-marital counseling. Sort of like taking a college CLEP test. I could picture this scenario:

CONCERNED OLDER PERSON: (approaches me) Hello, Michael. Congratulations on your engagement. Now you should stop by the church office to schedule a good number of counseling sessions with our preacher.

ME: Thank you, sir (or ma'am). I appreciate your fine suggestion, but you see, I have already attended the Brecheen/Faulkner Marriage Seminar. I think I am ready to be wed.

C.O.P: (nodding approvingly) Oh yes, Michael. As a Brecheen/Faulkner graduate, you should be fine. You should be just fine indeed.

Cheryl and I ended up devoting the better part of a weekend to the marriage seminar. I think it lasted about 74 hours. I'm not sure.

Paul Faulkner and Carl Brecheen took turns sharing the tricks of the marriage trade. I liked Faulkner better. (Sorry, Carl.) Brother Paul was like a friendly old uncle or grandpa. He told a bunch of stories. One of them involved details about a trip that he'd taken with his wife. For an entire day, Paul had done everything his wife wanted to do. EVERYTHING. Shopping? Sure, dear! Eating at a fancy restaurant? Absolutely! Time for some coffee and dessert afterwards? You bet, honey!

(I'm pretty sure Brother Faulkner got a little action after that trip. I'm just saying...)

Listening to Paul tell stories was the easy part. Having to do the participant exercises was a little more challenging.

For example, at one point during the Saturday session, everyone in the audience was supposed to hold the hand of his or her loved one, look him or her in the eyes and say something like: "I will always love you. I will never leave you. You are the most important person to me..."

It felt like about two steps beyond marriage vows. Honestly, Cheryl and I weren't quite ready for this. It was a little too soon and a little bit awkward.

But now, looking back after 20-plus years of this thing called marriage, I can pause and say, "I get it. I need to take care of my spouse. I need to cherish her. Brothers Brecheen and Faulkner had it exactly right."

Well, except for the part about shopping together.

———

Darin (b. 1972)

My parents used to take me along to the Tulsa Soul Winning Workshop. I liked wandering through the Expo building and looking at all the booths. There were about a thousand different types of Bibles being sold, and several a cappella groups would be singing and selling their tapes as well. A bunch of us kids would run around, playing in the open areas of the Expo building.

During the evening sessions, the singing in the Pavilion was extra loud and powerful, and the speakers were amazing. I loved Ronnie White's sermon about David and Goliath and was excited when my friend Clint was baptized.

Love and Marriage

A common prayer among parents in the church: *Dear Lord, please raise up our children to be strong Christians, and please help them to find Christian spouses one day.*

———

You might be Church of Christ if ... you were married in an A-frame building with paneled walls and red shag carpet.

———

We're smoking cigars in a dugout at Berryhill baseball field in Searcy. Doug and me, college freshman. The night is cool and wet. Drops of rain smack on the blocks of concrete that surround us. We are talking about women. Not an uncommon topic of conversation. We call it philosophizing, which apparently is a real word. It's a funny term, and we grin whenever we say it. "Philosophizing."

Tonight, we discuss what we want in a future mate.

Looks.

Personality.

Spirituality.

Doug offers some advice which comes from his Dad. "When you're looking for a girl to marry, look for a girl who goes to church AND to Bible class."

We think this is pretty good advice.

The only question we have: Are we ready to look for the girls we want to marry?

———

My bride & me.

When I think of our wedding day, I first think of our parents.

I know. It's weird.

Cheryl's dad standing straight and tall in a men's quartet at the front of the auditorium, belting out "God Give Us Christian Homes."

God, give us Christian homes!
Homes where the mother, in queenly quest,
Strives to show others Thy way is best,
Homes where the Lord is an honored guest...

My dad, sincerely preaching the wedding sermon, encouraging Cheryl not to work outside of the home, getting choked up in the middle of it all.

My mom, constantly patting me on the back and arms, quietly letting me know that I'd done good.

Cheryl's mom—before everything got started—shooing me out of the church building so I wouldn't see the bridal gown pass by.

I didn't see the dress on that morning, but I did spot my fiancée strolling across the parking lot.

Which always brings my thoughts back to where they should be. Where I spy the 22-year-old version of Cheryl moving between cars. Hair in rollers. Sweatpants.

In my mind's eye, I can still see it. Crisp. Clear. See it for what it was. See it for what it is. The beginning of the best chapters of my life.

———

Gary (b. 196X)

Just before I got married, the preacher from my church was fired. On my wedding day, the elders were handing out letters in the foyer to inform people of the ministry change.

Divorce and Remarriage

Dad used to talk about "The Divorce Question," a somewhat hot topic within the Church of Christ. (From time to time, he would also mention "The War Question," whether or not a Christian could join the military and fight in combat.) Dad believed there were situations where a person could be divorced and still be a member of the church.

Some other people we knew were not so open to the idea of divorced Christians. The most extreme view, held by some, was that a person should always try to reconcile with his or her first spouse, unless there was evidence of adultery.

———

My buddy John's mom split from his family. She took off for the bright lights of Nashville. I'm sure it was complicated.

On a long weekend trip through Tennessee, John and I stopped by for dinner with his mom. She looked young and fresh and fit, more like my friend's older sister than his mother. She told us stories about an exciting Michael Jackson concert and about feeling guilty when she ate too much pizza.

The entire evening was pretty awkward. I felt sorry for John ... and for his mom. All I could think was "How sad is this?"

———

Steve (b. 1963)

I grew up with the mindset that, if someone was divorced, then he or she was a bad person.

Thressea (b. 1963)

My parents divorced when I was in middle school. Afterward, the elders at our small congregation stepped in to help my mom, brother, and me. During one particularly difficult period, they came over to our house and replaced the roof.

I don't know what we'd have done without their support.

Women's Role in the Church

The Church of Christ did not allow a woman to have a position of authority over a man. This usually meant that women did not lead prayers, lead singing, or preach whenever men were present. Even less visible roles like serving communion and ushering were typically reserved for men only.

––––––––

Fresh out of college, I worked for two years at Central Arkansas Christian, a Church of Christ high school in North Little Rock, Arkansas. I taught P.E. and Bible.

One semester, my Bible classes were studying the book of First Corinthians, and I knew the topic of WOMEN'S ROLE IN THE CHURCH was coming up. (When I heard those words in my mind, it was a deep booming voice that kind of echoed.) For this topic, I knew I'd have to put in more prep time than my usual reading of a few paragraphs in *Halley's Bible Handbook.*

With that in mind, I grabbed a commentary or two that outlined the Church of Christ position on WOMEN'S ROLE. I also discussed the doctrine with my principal Bobby. I felt like I was building a Lincoln Log cabin, stacking up all of the arguments and scriptures, one on top of the other. I worried about questions the students might ask. I worried even more about the wrong answers I might give.

My thoughts played out like this ahead of time:

Excuse me, Coach Allen; the verse says a woman should keep silent in the church. Is it okay for a woman to speak up in a Sunday morning Bible class?

Um, Yes.

Is it okay for her to read a scripture in Bible class?

Yes. I think so.

Can she serve communion?

Uhhh...

What about reading announcements?

No. Wait. Maybe she could do it if she were in a sitting position and not exerting authority. Hold it. Is there a microphone? If there's a microphone involved, that could change things.

Could she lead singing?

No.

But in chorus, we have women who sing solos.

That's different.

How?

Next question.

Can a woman preach?

Absolutely not!

Okay, maybe I stressed a little too much in advance. I do know I had a lot of trouble figuring out what parts of the Bible involved cultural rules and what parts of the Bible outlined everlasting rules.

For example:

Holy kiss = cultural.

Women shouldn't braid their hair = cultural.

Women keep silent = everlasting.

But what about those four pesky daughters of Philip who prophesied in the book of Acts? And of course there was the Old Testament judge Deborah who led the whole nation of Israel.

It was all sort of confusing to me, but when the fateful day finally arrived, I was able to successfully teach the students and answer their questions. What a relief!

There was just one small problem, though. A week later, as I thought back, I couldn't seem to remember any of the arguments for WOMEN'S ROLE IN THE CHURCH. They flew right out of my brain like a flock of seagulls.

"Dang it!" I thought, "I'll have to memorize them all over again next year."

Ralph (b. 1944)

I believe it breaks God's heart that the Church of Christ has all these prohibitions against women. Women should be allowed to participate in all areas of church life – particularly in the area of leadership.

I've heard firsthand about the heartbreak of women who have been treated poorly or even ignored. Many young people have left the church because of this teaching. And they should leave … until we are willing to make a change.

Elisabeth (b. 193X)

I have seen the church change its positions on several things through the years (racial relations for example) and wonder about possible changes on the position of women's roles. (By the way, my daddy felt that it was all right for women to pray in public, but he did not push that idea on other Christians.) I have felt that women have been hogtied in some ways in the past, and now I have been glad to see women working on the church staff in several roles other than secretarial.

Instrumental Music

Although the Church of Christ has traditionally kept musical instruments out of the church building, many members do listen to contemporary Christian music outside of the church.

Some (typically older) members still consider worshipping with "instrumental music" to be wrong.

————

My brother was walking around the house one day in his underwear. He was being silly, singing a gospel song and snapping his waistband to the beat.

"Oooh, Jimmy," I said. "That's instrumental music."

It was my first sarcastic church joke.

————

Ode to Amy Grant.

I loved Amy Grant. Not in a "crush" kind of way, but in a "big sister" kind of way. In 1981, Amy was the only contemporary Christian musician I'd ever heard of. Were there others?

During my 10th grade year, my girlfriend Rosemary made me a couple of bootleg Amy Grant tapes. They were awesome, with songs like "Father's Eyes" and "Old Man's Rubble." I used to listen to Amy every morning before school. And, in doing so, I started feeling closer to God. In a way, after years of hearing mostly hymns in an a-cappella-only format, Amy's music was like switching from black-and-white to color television.

Don't get me wrong. I still liked some of the old standards, such as "Come, Ye that Love the Lord" and "How Shall the Young Secure Their Hearts." But there were times at church, maybe before communion, when I thought, "I'm not sure if I can sing another verse of 'When I Survey the Wondrous Cross.'"

Amy put a little juice back into my spiritual life.

———

Someone told me about a minister who had worn Groucho Marx glasses (with plastic nose and mustache) to an Amy Grant concert. The minister joked that he was in disguise so that no one would recognize him at the show.

———

My dad wrote a book titled *Instrumental Music in Worship.*

In it, he explains the traditional Church of Christ view of having no musical instruments in a worship service. It's an important issue for him.

One day, I baited him at the dining room table.

MIKE: Dad, do you think it's EVER alright to play a musical instrument with a church song?

DAD: No, I don't think that instrumental music should ever accompany a church song.

MIKE: Okay. (Dramatic pause.) Did you know that some of the choruses at Harding practice their music with a piano? Do you think that's wrong?

DAD: Yes, I believe that's wrong.

MIKE: Then, why don't you go talk to them about it? (Silence.)

MIKE: If they're doing something wrong, then why don't you go talk to them about it, Dad?

DAD: I'm not going to talk to them about it.

(Silence.)

———

One day, my co-worker Stacey and I were talking about churches located in Austin, TX. She said, "We visited this one church. The people there were so friendly, but there was no music!"

I knew exactly what she was talking about. Hymns

were sung, but there was no organ or piano.

I smiled and pointed at Stacey, "That, my friend, is a Church of Christ."

Warm people. No musical instruments.

Dennis (b. 1956)

Listening to contemporary Christian music has been a great comfort to our family. I could list dozens of songs and artists that have helped us along the way. I consider many of these songs to be modern-day psalms.

I should add that I'm not trying to change our tradition of a cappella singing in the worship assembly, but I do not believe that "instrumental music" is a salvation issue.

Gary (b. 196X)

I asked my Bible class teacher, "Why do we say you can't use instruments in worship?"

The teacher sighed and replied, "That question was settled in our church many years ago. We aren't going to waste time discussing something that won't change anyway, so let's move on."

I thought, "But I wasn't even born when all that was decided! Why can't we talk about it now?"

Ralph (b. 1944)

My parents argued over religion.   Mother said, "I will not go to the Church of Christ and hear the preacher condemn me for using an organ in worship."

So they compromised, and our family joined the Christian Church in town.

Black and White

The Church of Christ was never fully integrated. In a number of towns—even very small ones—it was not uncommon for there to be a "white" church and also a "black" church.

A mixed-married couple—a white woman and a black man—were members of the College Church during my teen years. I thought, "Why would they want to be married to one another? They stick out like a sore thumb."

Years later, I met lots of racially-mixed couples in the military. I thought, "Oh, this is no big deal. Why was I so uptight about it before?"

In the spring of 1989, I worked as a student teacher at Harding Academy. One day I was asked to referee a 7th grade boys' basketball game. The team playing against Harding wore practice jerseys without numbers. One of the boys from the other school was a tall and solidly-built African American student. The first time I called a foul on him, I walked over the scorer's table and said, "That was a foul on the big black boy." A little bit later, I whistled him again. This time I yelled over to the scorer's table, "Hey, foul on the black boy!"

One of the Harding Academy coaches motioned me over. He put a hand on my shoulder and said softly, "Mike, you probably don't want to be calling him 'black boy.' That could be embarrassing for him."

My face flushed. I hadn't even thought about it. I nodded and jogged back onto the court.

Ralph (b. 1944)

As a freshman at Harding College, my roommate Jerry and I volunteered for a campaign in Hazen, Arkansas. The people in charge forgot to tell us not to invite black people to the gospel meeting, so we went throughout the black neighborhoods inviting folks. One man named John came to the meeting, but was not allowed inside the church building because of his race. Jerry and I were stunned.

It still makes me angry when I think about that time.

Gary (b. 196X)

It was always stated that we welcomed black people at church, but they never came, and I wondered how welcome they really felt. We were quick to say it wasn't a racial thing, but I decided pretty early on it was a racial thing.

Denise (196X)

The Wilsons were the only black family at our church.

Mr. Wilson was a big man with a deep booming voice. He always kept a close eye on the kids in the church lobby, reminding us that running was not allowed. And we never ran, at least not while Mr. Wilson was watching. Mrs. Wilson was a tiny woman with a warm smile and kind personality. They had three children; the youngest of the three was an adopted son who had special needs.

One weekend, our family decided to invite the Wilsons over for dinner. Before they arrived, though, my parents told my sisters and me not to tell our grandparents about the visit. Even though we all went to the same church, my parents worried about how my granddad would react to us having a black family into our home.

Dennis (b. 1944)

Perhaps the most wrenching realization I experienced during my college years had to do with civil rights. As I became gradually convinced of the sin of racial prejudice and especially racial exploitation, I had to reconsider the morality of the culture--even the church culture--in which I had been nurtured. I've never forgotten the shame I felt for my complicity in this social evil.

Recognizing how well-meaning, spiritual people can

be blind to their flaws made me thereafter more hesitant to accept "church" authority and more tolerant of other Christians who might disagree with us on doctrinal points. Indeed, everyone falls short.

What about the Baptists?

One primary distinction between the Church of Christ and the Baptist Church was the teaching about a person's salvation. The Baptists believed a person was saved at the moment of coming to faith in Jesus Christ. The Church of Christ typically held that an individual was saved at the point of baptism (immersion in water).

———

When I was a young teen, Jerry Jones (a Harding Bible professor) and my dad appeared on "The John Ankerberg Show," a religious television talk show. They sat on an enormous stage somewhere in Chattanooga, Tennessee and debated a couple of distinguished-looking men who believed that baptism was not essential for salvation. John Ankerberg, an ordained Baptist minister with an amazing head full of blond hair, moderated the discussion.

The other guys didn't stand a chance. They stuttered and stammered and looked to Mr. Ankerberg for help.

On the opposite side of the aisle, Jerry and Dad appeared cool and confident. They steadily hammered away at all the Baptists' arguments.

As a somewhat biased viewer, I thought they had kicked some Baptist butt.

———

In high school I had a date with a Baptist minister's daughter. She was warm, friendly and quite chatty. I liked her. I brought her home to meet my parents. She was completely charming with them.

Sometime later, Dad invited her father, the Baptist minister, to visit a School of Biblical Studies class at Harding. (SBS was a part of Harding specifically set apart to train preachers.) In the class, the students had a question-and-answer time with the minister. Many of the questions centered on whether or not a person had to be baptized to be saved. Dad said the minister was very gracious in his answers. Afterward, Dad and the minister walked and talked for awhile together.

I could see that my father was torn. Here was a Searcy family that he felt some affection for, but he had trouble fully accepting them because of their doctrine.

———

(An old joke.)

Saint Peter and a newly-arrived Baptist are walking along the golden streets of heaven. As they pass through one section, Peter asks the Baptist to keep his voice down.

"Why do you want me to do that?" the Baptist asks.

Peter replies, "Because this is where the Church of Christ members live, and they think they're the only ones here."

Mary (b. 195X)

We are getting better now, but in the '60s and '70s, we weren't very nice to believers outside of the churches of Christ.

Shanna (b.1982)

When I was in middle school, one of the elders at church was my Bible class teacher. I asked him one time if he thought my friend Ashley, who went to a Baptist church, would go to heaven. He said "Ultimately the decision is up to God, but her church doesn't follow the Bible as closely as we do, so I don't know if she will."

Jeff (b. 1958)

Growing up, I felt that other religious groups were sort of the "enemy" and that they purposefully twisted the scriptures.

Britt (b. 1968)

My parents viewed church doctrine as important, but

our family regularly associated with people outside of the Church of Christ. At times, my dad taught adult classes at a local Baptist church, and I also attended some Methodist and Baptist-sponsored youth events (which included a few dances).

No-nos

The Church of Christ tended to frown upon certain "worldly" activities. These included drinking alcohol, smoking, gambling, dancing and mixed swimming.

———

Bywords.

In elementary school, we thought some bywords were bad words.

Words like: gee, gosh, golly, darn, and drat.

There was a song I liked on my family's *Up with People III* album. It was called "Gee, I'm Looking Forward to the Future."

I felt a little guilty when I listened to that song.

There was also a Disney movie I liked called *That Darn Cat*. Kids in my grade didn't want to say the middle word, so at recess we asked each other if we'd seen "That D.C."

Speaking of recess, I got in trouble one day for something my mouth said. Big trouble. I got mad at Brian and yelled, "Go suck an egg!" I didn't know what it meant. (I'm still not sure what it means.) The recess monitor—the tall one with brown hair who I had a crush on—came over and said that telling someone to "suck an egg" was a very bad thing to do. I had to apologize to Brian, even though he didn't seem very offended by it.

Now that I think about it, Brian might be the kid who taught me that particular phrase.

————

In 1997, I had a 9-month Air Force assignment to San Angelo, TX, a city with two large Churches of Christ. Our family visited both churches, deciding to place membership at the one where we knew another couple from our Harding days. The preacher at this church was a big mustached man who wore cowboy boots with his suit. He reminded us of John Wayne, except he wanted to save the Indians (not kill them). He told us inspirational stories of baptisms. We liked this guy.

After a few months at church, a woman approached Cheryl and me, asking if we'd be willing to teach a Bible class. "Sure," we said, and the woman handed us a two-sided form to fill out. Now this was a more formal process than what we'd seen in the past. At other places, people would walk up to us and say, "You wanna teach?" and the next week we'd be cutting out pictures of Noah's ark in the classroom. This time, we had to successfully navigate a bunch of questions first.

I got stuck on the second page.

What is your view of dancing?

Hmmm. I really hadn't thought much about this one before. What was my view of dancing? Well, I had been involved in "Spring Sing" in college. There we performed some cool choreography. Did that count? And I guess that dancing with my spouse was okay. Right? And wasn't there an example of someone dancing in the Bible? No, I don't mean that woman who danced for Herod, but you know, King David, dancing before the Lord. He was a good guy, wasn't he? So, yeah, I thought that dancing was probably an okay thing for a Christian to do.

Cheryl and I turned in our applications and waited for a call back. It never came. I think my dancing answer sunk our chances.

And that was alright with me. Seriously. You see, I didn't really want to teach a Bible class anyway.

────────

Donald (b. 195X)

Everything was black and white. You never heard the expression, "I disagree with you, but I could be wrong." Nope, it was simply, "You are wrong," or maybe, "You are dead wrong."

Mary (b. 195X)

One Bible class teacher had us sign up to be a part of the "No Smoke, No Drink Club." We even had membership cards.

Phil (b. 1956)

I went forward to be baptized because I just knew I was going to hell for betting 10 cents on a baseball game.

Ralph (b. 1944)

I wish I had learned to dance as a teenager.

Dancing is immensely enjoyable, but learning to do it as an adult has required a great deal of tolerance on the part of my wife.

Rock and Roll

During the 1980s, one popular topic among Church of Christ youth groups seemed to be "The Evils of Rock and Roll." Some youth ministers and other well-meaning adults spent a good amount of time telling students about satanic messages and sexual content found in the pop music of that time.

———

A few of us asked a Bible class teacher, "What kind of music should we be listening to?"

He thought about it for a moment and then recommended the soundtrack for *The Sound of Music* or possibly some Beethoven.

———

In high school, one of our teachers taught us about the dangers of "backmasking." Backmasking evidently happened when a rock band included backwards lyrics (sometimes "satanic" ones) in a song in order to influence young minds. Our teacher told us that groups like the Beatles, Led Zeppelin, and Queen had all done it.

I recognized some of the songs he was talking about, but I hadn't realized there were backward messages inside of them.

After the class, my friend Michael and I went back to his house. We must have listened to Led Zeppelin's "Stairway to Heaven" about a hundred times ... backwards.

Our teacher was right; there were some very interesting things in there.

————

I traveled down to Little Rock's Barton Coliseum for a bunch of rock concerts when I was in high school and college. I saw Styx, Loverboy, Joan Jett and the Blackhearts, Foreigner, Huey Lewis and the News, and Cheap Trick.

During the shows, I would sometimes think, "Man, I hope Jesus doesn't return tonight. I might be in trouble."

————

Rain on the Scarecrow.

I liked John Cougar Mellencamp, but I hated that song.

Now, I know John was singing to help the farmers, but the guitar parts hurt my ears. And there's blood on the farm equipment? What does that mean!?

I could not listen to that song.

Until one day, when I saw the video of it on MTV. In the final scenes, John and his boy band were jamming on the front steps of a small white church building. The sign over the door said BELMONT CHURCH of CHRIST.

———————

Rebekah (b. 1971)

A couple of the high school teachers made us listen to the song "Hotel California" by the Eagles. We heard it frontward and backward. The teachers said we shouldn't be listening to this evil music because there were hidden "cult" messages in it. This made me wonder why the teachers had played the song for us in the first place.

I learned later that the Eagles were talking about drugs instead of a secret cult.

Sin

According to the Bible, we have all sinned and fallen short of the glory of God. We have sinned by breaking the commands of God and by failing to do the good stuff God intended for us to do.

The Church of Christ provided a means of publicly confessing sin where a person could come forward during the invitation song for "restoration." The responding person would usually write out comments on a card or have a confession pre-written. An elder, deacon, or other leading man in the church would then read the information to the congregation and pray for the individual. The response might be pretty generic, "I have sinned and ask for your prayers," or it could be more specific, mentioning a premarital pregnancy or the loss of temper during a basketball game.

Of course, private confession could also take place among trusted friends or with a minister.

————

In elementary school, we'd usually have a Friday morning "hymn sing" led by our music teacher Mrs. Henry. Sometimes, Mrs. Henry would take suggestions from the students, saying something like, "Okay, today we'll take requests from the fourth grade." One of our very favorite songs included the words "Gloria in Excelsis Deo" which was sung in a rolling melody as Glo-O-o-o-o-o-O-o-o-o-o-O-o-o-o-o-ria! We asked for that song all the time.

On some Fridays, dads of students would drop by to lead the singing. On one such morning, Mr. P was standing up front and taking a few requests. One kid in the back of the auditorium raised his hand and asked for "Love Lifted Me." Mr. P turned to the number in his blue, *Great Songs of The Church* song book. He paused and said soberly, "You know, I'm not sure the first verse of this song really applies to this group. Let's take a look at it together."

He read slowly from the page, and we all followed along with him,

I was sinking deep in sin, far from the peaceful shore,

Very deeply stained within, sinking to rise no more,
But the master of the sea, heard my despairing cry,
From the waters lifted me, now safe am I.

He glanced back up at us and said, "You see, I'm not sure you all can sing this verse and mean it. You were raised in Christian homes. You have not experienced 'sinking deep in sin.' You do not understand what that is like. So why don't we just begin with the second verse instead?"

And so we sang the second verse:

All my heart to him I give, ever to him I'll cling,
In his blessed presence live, ever his praises sing,
Love so mighty and so true, merits my soul's best
songs,
Faithful, loving service too, to him belongs.

Thinking back on that morning, so long ago, I believe Mr. P had it right. We weren't sinking deep in sin. We weren't deeply stained within. The first verse really didn't apply to us.

But I wonder sometimes. What about now? All of these years later?

———

We, the members of the College Church, were involved in boycotts and protests in order to combat sin.

Polite protests.

There was a time, maybe around 1980, when a spate of sexually suggestive programs came on TV. Maybe shows like *Dallas* and *Dynasty*, I'm not sure.

And the elders said, we are going to write letters and we are not going to buy products from companies who run commercials on these shows.

And the elders handed out a list of companies that we weren't going to buy things from for awhile. And some

of the companies were huge—like Procter & Gamble—
and sold good stuff that we used every day. But we were
willing to change our toothpaste or whatever because it was
the right thing to do.

And later (or before) there was a convenience store in
town that wanted to sell dirty magazines out on racks, and
the elders said we are going to boycott that store unless
there is a change. And since a ton of the customers were
churchgoers who hated dirty magazines, the store manager
decided to change the policy. And the mags stayed behind
the counter where no one could see them.

And I think about those times where we made a stand
for what was right. And I feel proud of what we did.

———

I'm a kid in Searcy, out for a bike ride on a warm and
sunny day.

I stop by my friend Randy's house. I knock on the door,
the side door. No one answers. I knock a few more times.
I'm sure now that no one is home. I turn to leave and see
boxes and boxes of fireworks stacked in the carport. Fireworks, which Randy's family sells in the summer, sitting
right out in the open for easy taking. I want some of them.
Badly. My fingers itch. My throat goes dry. I feel pulled,
like I'm caught in the tractor beam of a spaceship. I look

around. No one would ever know. I want the expensive ones, the rockets and giant Roman candles, but instead, I slowly turn to leave. I will myself away. Maybe it's the fear of getting caught. Maybe it's something else. I'm not sure. I hop on my bike and quickly ride toward home.

I'm an adult in Falls Church, Virginia, out for a bike ride on a warm and sunny day.

I come up a short hill and turn right into a driveway. Someone else's driveway. I stop here, as I normally do, before crossing a busy road. I take a long drink of water and catch my breath. I notice the trees on both sides of the driveway which block the view of passing motorists. I see the house sitting far away in the distance. On this little piece of pavement, everything is still. I look down and notice a copy of The Washington Post wrapped in plastic. The Sunday edition. Untouched. Pristine. I want it. My fingers itch and my throat goes dry. I am certain that no one would ever know. I think about scooping it up and speeding away with the newspaper dangling from my handlebars. I hesitate and hear the sound of a car, very close, turning into the driveway. I smile and wave at the driver, before riding off toward home.

———

I swear sometimes. It's embarrassing. I could blame it on all of my years in the military, but that's not really a good excuse.

Before I went into the Air Force, way back in 1990, the preacher from my church in Little Rock called me into his office. "Mike," he said, "Have you ever been in a public school locker room? Well, they use some pretty rough language in there, and that's how it's going to be in the military." He was trying to change my mind—to keep me from joining. It didn't work, but he was right about the swearing thing. There was quite a lot of it.

So from time to time, when I get frustrated or angry. I think swear words. Sometimes I whisper the swear words. And every once in a while, the swear comes out loud. Full force. Forte!!! I feel guilty and wish it would stop.

Let me give you an example. At home one day, my son Cal accidentally dropped a can of Lysol onto my wife's noggin. (It's a long story, and yes, there was bleeding involved.) I turned from my desk in time to see it happen. "@#$%!," I shouted. It was the kind of swear word that would have gotten me stoned in the camp of the Israel-ites. A really, really bad one. My kids heard me. I felt so ashamed. A few minutes later, after getting a bandage for my wife's forehead, I apologized to my entire family.

I'd like to say that, since that day, I have never ever said another bad word out loud. But unfortunately that's not the truth. The fact is that I'm working on it. Most of the time, I'm doing okay, but sometimes I still slip up. I'm weak. I need God's help and mercy.

Feel free to pray for me if you like.

————

Sean (b. 196X)

When I was a kid, there was a man at our church who brought a stack of pornographic magazines over to our house and confessed his sins to my father. Later, Daddy put the magazines in our living room to go out with the morning trash. I looked at a couple of them.

As I got older, I had my own problems with pornography. I was married with kids, and I finally talked it over with a couple of guys from church. One of them said, "You need to repent!" I did, but it was a hard thing to do.

I have been porn-free for several years now.

Rebuking

Some people were quick to speak words of encouragement during times of teaching or training. Others saw weakness and moved too swiftly, too freely, toward rebuke.

———

At the back of the church building, near some stairs that led to the balcony, I noticed a silver-haired man who was lecturing a boy from my school.

"Son, you need to put on your best clothes for Sunday. You need to show God your best. Do you understand?"

The boy didn't say anything. He just nodded.

I didn't know the man's name, but I knew his wife always wore a veil to church. Not a cover-your-face veil, but a sit-on-top-of-your-head veil. A lacy thing that looked like something my grandma would use to decorate a couch.

And standing right here in front of me, this three-piece-suit guy was scolding a youngster who'd worn jeans to church.

Did the man know anything about the boy? Did he realize the boy didn't have a father at home?

———

Our family attended a church in Hawaii that wasn't

doing so well. Many people were leaving, and after awhile, our preacher Peter stepped down. He couldn't take the pressure anymore.

A few days later, I attended a small group leaders' meeting where our interim minister asked us an out-of-the-blue question.

"What was the first thing that popped into your head when you heard Peter was leaving?"

Silence.

I spoke up. "The first thing that popped into my head? I thought, good. He's leaving. He was doing a lousy job."

The minister spent the next 10 minutes chastising me, telling me I needed to change my attitude.

After the meeting, a friend caught up to me in the lobby. "Are you okay?" he asked.

———

Craig (b. 1955)

When I was a sophomore or junior in high school, our youth group started singing songs spontaneously in the auditorium before the church services began. After the second or third Sunday of this, a man asked the elders if he could address the congregation at the start of the evening assembly. At that time, he proceeded to berate the youth for trying to act like a church choir. No elder, not a single one, ever publicly stood up for us.

There were a couple of teenagers who never came back after that.

Shanna (b.1982)

One year, after a Youth in Action convention, my friend decided to be baptized at a Sunday evening church service. When she came up out of the water, our youth group clapped for her (as we had done at YIA). We were later reprimanded for this at a meeting with the elders.

Withdrawing Fellowship

On rare occasions, elders would "withdraw fellowship" from a church member who was involved in a continuing-sin issue. Withdrawing fellowship was considered to be a last resort in helping the person repent (turn) from his or her sin. Typically, other church members were not supposed to socialize with the disfellowshipped person until full repentance had been displayed.

———

The College Church elders disfellowshipped a few people in the late 1970s or early 1980s. Whenever it happened, an elder would publicly read an announcement to the congregation. It seemed like the sin issue was always adultery.

The people who lost membership, as far as I could tell, weren't coming to church anymore. It was awfully embarrassing for their families who were left behind. Some of their kids were about my age.

———

I was riding along in a car one afternoon with an Air Force friend. He mentioned that his dad had been disfellowshipped years earlier. "After that, I always felt like the bastard son of Bill Watson," my friend said.

———

Steve (b. 1963)

I came from an area in Texas that was dominated by the engineering profession. Most of our church leaders were engineers. They were strong on common sense, but sometimes short on emotion, compassion, grace and forgiveness.

When the elders decided to disfellowship someone, it was a huge deal. It happened a few times in our church.

A Touch of Grace

Grace was taught at times and expressed at times, but in my estimation, there wasn't quite enough of it. We needed to feel more grace, from God and from other Christians, for our sins and for our mistakes.

————

About a year out of college, I took a job working as a part-time youth minister for a small Church of Christ in Little Rock, Arkansas. I made $150 a week in the summer and $75 a week during the school year. It gave a nice little boost to my teaching salary.

Our big trip that first summer was to St. Louis. We'd had a smooth weekend and were heading back home on a hazy Sunday afternoon. My wife Cheryl rode in the front passenger seat of our white church van, and we had 8 or so teenagers packed into the back. Traffic was heavy that day, and I was nervous we might not make it back to Little Rock in time for the evening worship service. I quickly pulled off the highway to get some gas.

After paying our bill, I looked across the lot to see the van gently rocking back and forth. What the heck? All of a sudden, one of the back windows just exploded, like a gunshot. Glass flew out onto the service station pavement.

I ran over and looked inside. Jerry, a high school senior, grinned out sheepishly, "Uh, me and Roger were wrassling." More details followed. Apparently, Jerry had placed his buttocks on the window for some extra leverage.

I thought, "Oh, man, I'm in big trouble. How did I let this happen?"

Cheryl and I covered the gaping hole with a large black garbage bag. It flapped like a buzzard as we drove back to the main road. I knew I'd have to stop soon and tell our preacher Bill about the accident. A short time later, I braced myself and dialed the number from a Pizza Hut payphone.

Bill picked up after a couple of rings. "Well, hello Michael. What's going on?" He pronounced my name Mackel, like the fish mackerel, but without the "er" sound.

"Hey, Bill, I've got some bad news. Um, first of all, we aren't going to make it back in time for the 6 o'clock church service. And also, um, we busted out a window in the church van."

I paused, not knowing what to expect.

"Now, Mackel. Don't you even worry about that. You all get back here when you can. We'll get the van fixed up this week. It's no big deal."

Ah, the cool breeze of grace. Now, all these summers later, I think back and say, "Thank you Brother Bill. That's just what I needed."

In fact, I still need it.

———

Jeff (b. 1958)

My youth group really changed my life. I always felt accepted and valued there.

Britt (b. 1968)

No single religious denomination is going to score 100% on the doctrine test. That is where I believe grace comes in to help us through.

A Church Divided

There are divisions within the Church of Christ. No surprise here. Sometimes Christians disagree.

———

I noticed a difference in doctrine, for the first time, on a summer trip when I was 16. My brother and I visited a "Non-institutional" Church of Christ in Florida. Non-institutional churches (a.k.a. "anti-cooperation" or "anti" churches) believed that it was wrong for one congregation to work with another congregation in support of a cause. In other words, two or more churches could not pool their money together in order to support an orphanage. Also, these churches tended to believe that people could not eat in the church building.

Why did they believe these things? I'm not sure.

———

At the Sunday evening service of an anti-cooperation church, the preacher talked about how only a small number of people in the world actually believed in the firm autonomy of each individual congregation. "But that's okay," he said, "because the Bible says only a few will be saved."

Wait a minute. Did he just say what I thought he said?

To be saved I had to be a member of an anti church?

"Oh well," I thought, "I guess I'll just have to take my chances."

———

Another split-off from the church became known as the "International" Church of Christ. I attended and eventually worked for the ICOC for several years in my 30s. This group placed a good amount of emphasis on discipleship, personal evangelism, and church growth. I enjoyed some wonderful relationships there and felt a renewed love for God's word and prayer.

I also became pretty judgmental. My bad for that.

———

I'm stuck in a discussion group at a ministry-staff meeting in central Connecticut. Sunlight streams through the windows of our second-floor meeting room, a space filled with male and female staff members from the Springfield Church, the Groton Church, and the Hartford Church. We sit in folding chairs, about six of us in each ragged circle. We're sharing goals for the upcoming season.

I'm feeling a little weary, a little burned out as an assistant minister. I believe I need to speak up about personal evangelism goals, but my heart is just not in it. My voice is flat.

Then, for some reason, I begin sharing about how I'm writing my own "Harmony of the Gospels," about how I am attempting to smoosh the books of Matthew, Mark, Luke and John into one smooth-flowing story. A couple of guys in my group perk up. They ask me some questions and seem genuinely interested.

I discover something on this fine morning. I find that this is where the "heat" is for me. Here is the passion. Not in numbers or in carefully laid plans, but in the story of Jesus Christ.

———

At an ICOC leaders' meeting, a minister spoke up and said, "Maybe we need to stop using the phrase 'We are the one true church, and there is no other.'"

Thankfully, everyone seemed to agree.

———

Steven (b. 1967)

After one year at Abilene Christian University, I transferred to Northeastern University in Boston. While there, I became a member of the Boston Church of Christ (a part of the ICOC) and experienced a time of real growth and close friendships. Over time, the church became legalistic, but many people there continued to genuinely love God and give their hearts to Him.

Later On

Hard Times

Jesus said we'd have storms in our lives, that the rains would come down and the floods would come up.

———

I lost my job in the summer of 2003. I'd been working as an assistant minister for a church in Connecticut. In the spring of that year, we had taken a long hard look at the budget at one of our staff meetings. The numbers didn't look so good. I knew it was just a matter of time before I'd have to go.

After the budget meeting, I scrambled to get my teaching license back. I got the certificate, but no job, so I took a substitute teaching position at a local middle school. It was miserable. Not every day, but most days. I actually looked forward to the times when I could help clean up the library or do some data entry in the school office. Trying to keep a rowdy 8th grade class under control—that was brutal.

I have a couple of strong memories from that time. I admit that the first one is strange.

I would drive to school in the mornings, twisting and turning through some neighborhoods before getting onto Interstate 84. Just before the highway, I would sit for awhile at a traffic light, waiting to turn left. At the intersection, my stomach would churn, and I'd be filled with dread for the coming day. Then I'd have this thought, "This must be how Jesus felt when he went to the cross." (I told you it was strange.)

The second event was more normal, I think. I was substituting in an 8th grade English class one afternoon. The students were "working" on projects in small groups. As I shuffled by one group, a sweet and chatty 8th grade girl looked up at me and said, "Mr. Allen, you look so sad."

I had no words for her. No witty response. I was sad. I looked at her, smiled weakly and kept moving.

———

My wife was attacked on a walking trail near our home. A 20-something guy came up behind her and tried to pull down her shorts. She screamed, and the guy ran away.

Afterward, counseling and prayer helped, but the wound remains. I can see it sometimes. A little bit of fear. The way she never walks down that path alone anymore. The way she carries a cell phone everywhere, just in case. Where would we be without the Lord in all of this?

———

Marty (b. 1966)

My wife was sick for a long time.

I finally began to understand that I was not in control, that I could not "fix" her. I was utterly dependent on God.

Lawana (b. 1944)

In our church family, we laugh together, we cry together and sometimes we even fight with each other. One day, I might be helping someone else, and the next day, I might be the one who needs some help in return.

I know my husband and I would not have survived the aftermath of our son's car accident without the love and support of our brothers and sisters in Christ.

Dennis (b. 1956)

We have tried to move forward, walking with God through our recent tragedy. The death of our daughter Micah helped us place a new emphasis on what's really important in life.

Micah was faithful in her relationship with God to the very end. We know this because of her prayer journal.

Thressea (b. 1963)

While working on the farm—milking cows, planting corn, cleaning out the barn—my grandfather taught my cousins and me all about the Bible. The most important lesson he shared with us: Always grasp the hand of God in difficult times.

He's been gone seven years now. I miss him, but I still gain strength from the memory of his love.

Staying

Sometimes people grow up in the Church of Christ, and they decide to stay put.

Janet (b. 195X)

My husband and I grew up in the churches of Christ, and we spent our first years of marriage working in campus ministry. I had not really experienced the "negative side" of my heritage until this time of life. While in campus ministry, we felt the struggle between conservative doctrines and dealing in people's lives which could be messy.

We eventually moved to Georgia where we were influenced by studying Experiencing God by Henry Blackaby and by attending seminars at the Willow Creek Community Church in the Chicago area. At about the same time, I accepted a job at an interdenominational school housed in a Presbyterian church. All of this opened our eyes to a much wider Christian world, seeing that people with other religious beliefs had not "parked their brains." I began to understand how others might see our church as a group who thought they had all the right answers and knew the only way to heaven.

Today, I remain in a "church of Christ," although most

would say it's a progressive one. I absolutely love instrumental praise and worship music, so I'd probably be the most comfortable, if attending another church, in a Christian or community church. My list of essentials in what it takes to unite Christians is much smaller than it used to be, and it doesn't require being a member of another church of Christ. What's essential is belief in Jesus Christ for salvation and having a personal walk with Him, living for Him in obedience every day and, hopefully, finding joy in the journey.

Shanna (b.1982)

My thinking differs from ideas you would find in most conservative churches, but I do still attend and love the church of Christ.

Rees (b. 1982)

I had a great childhood in the church I grew up in, but as I got older my experiences there became less and less great.

I eventually found what I was looking for in another church of Christ that was more outreach-minded.

Rick (b. 1968)

I first attended a Church of Christ when I was about

14. I had grown up Baptist, but had never gone anywhere regularly. During that first service, I remember the singing, especially the song "Our God He is Alive." I thought it was the coolest music I'd ever heard. From that day on, the College Avenue Church seemingly raised me.

I started going to church with my friend Alan who had invited me about a hundred times. I finally ran out of excuses not to come. Besides, I'd met a cute girl there and decided that maybe church wasn't such a bad thing after all.

The congregation accepted me immediately, giving me lots of time to grow and learn in a supportive environment. There was a group of men there—probably in their 20s and 30s—who took a special interest in me and my friends. They'd play basketball with us and would often ask us about how things were going in school. They offered lots of encouragement along the way.

I became a Christian in August of 1984. Alan was within days of leaving for college, and we were up late one Saturday night talking. He said, "I don't feel like I can leave for school knowing that you're not a Christian." The next day we talked to our youth minister, and I was baptized that afternoon in front of several families and the youth group.

There were so many people in that first congregation who looked out for me. One person, Charles, would often visit Harding University, and he always found an excuse to take me along. Later, when I enrolled at Harding, a couple from College Avenue paid a large portion of my college expenses.

I am so incredibly grateful for this wonderful group of Christians who stepped in when I desperately needed a spiritual family. Although I attend another Church of Christ now, my College Avenue "family" has continued to care for me for almost 30 years.

Lance (b. 1966)

In all of the different places I've lived, I always tried early on to find a good church home. It would have been so easy to slip away, being out there on my own.

Thressea (b. 1963)

The Church of Christ is my life. My family and closest friendships are there. I can't imagine where I would be without the Church.

Leaving

Sometimes people grow up in the Church of Christ and end up going off to another church after 20 or 30 or 40 or more years. And sometimes the question lingers in the back of their minds:

Is it really okay to leave?

———

I was talking to an old family friend about people who had left the Church of Christ. He said, "Michael, what you've got to understand is, that for some people, going away is a matter of spiritual survival."

———

Leaving.

Is that okay? To leave the Church of Christ? I wonder sometimes.

I left. Maybe this desire to leave started when I went to the International Church of Christ. Maybe it began much before that. Like when I began listening to Amy Grant's music or when I attended a gospel chapel service at Maxwell Air Force Base. I'm not sure. But I did leave.

In the summer of 2004...

...our family moved from Connecticut to Falls Church,

Virginia. Actually, I moved first. About 3 weeks before the rest of my crew. I came down. Worked. Scoped out the area. And then Cheryl, Kate and Cal joined me in August.

We had it in our minds to settle in and to begin looking for a church. And we prayed. Hard. All Churches of Christ were "on the table." Traditional. International. Liberal. But we had an idea in the back of our minds of what we wanted. We wanted a church that was a little more gracey and a little less rulesy. A church where we could catch a glimpse of God and His love and encouragement. A place to fill up our somewhat depleted emotional tanks.

We started by visiting an International Church of Christ. This one met in a local high school, and we attended two Wednesdays and two Sundays.

It was the 2nd Wednesday that killed us. It was then that we knew that this was not the church for us. In fact, I was surprised on that night to find out that it was the church for anyone. On that fateful Wednesday night, the man teaching the adult Bible class went off. O-F-F.

Let me explain. Evidently, the previous Sunday, the entire church had traveled down the road to Richmond—100 miles away—for an all-Virginia church service. So the regular members (not our family) had hopped into cars, driven for 2 hours one-way, endured a longish church service, stayed after for a potluck meal, and had then driven two hours home.

I thought everyone who had made the trip deserved a shiny medal and a great big hug. Wow! That was some dedication.

But the middle-aged guy who was leading the Wednesday night Bible class had a different opinion. He stood up at the front of the auditorium, and very seriously, very intensely, started talking about the all-Virginia church service. Evidently, he had a problem, an issue that needed to be worked through. And it was time to confront the Wednesday night crowd. His issue was that some people— some of the people who had driven down to Richmond, who had sat through the longish church service, who had attended the potluck lunch, and who had driven 2 hours in order to get back home—some of those people HAD NOT DONE A VERY GOOD JOB OF FELLOWSHIPPING WITH OTHER CHRISTIANS AT THE POTLUCK!

I write that in all caps because he was speaking in all caps. I thought to myself, "What in the world is he talking about?"

Then came the line, the line that burned itself into my brain. This guy said, "Now when you get to heaven (pause), IF YOU MAKE IT TO HEAVEN (pause), who are you going to talk to? Are you just going to sit around by yourself?"

I thought this was possibly the most ridiculous thing I had heard in my entire church-going life. Could I be a part of a church where this was said? Where this was tolerated? Where a person's salvation might be called into question because he or she did a poor job of fellowshipping at a potluck meal?

My heart was racing. My chest didn't stop aching, even an hour and a half later when I was safely home in bed. I thought, "This ain't the church for me." (I use the word "ain't" when I'm angry.) Cheryl felt the same way.

And so we kept searching.

We visited a couple of other more traditional Churches of Christ. We found the people at these churches to be very kind and warm. Easily some of the friendliest people we had met in Virginia. But the content there no longer fit us well.

Let me try to explain.

As one example, Cheryl and I went to a Sunday morning Bible class at the _____ Church of Christ. The topic of the class was on having great quiet times with God. We thought, "Excellent. This is exactly what we need to hear." But the members of the class ended up having an extended discussion on whether or not it was okay to listen to instrumental worship music during a quiet time or at any other time. I thought, "I can't do this anymore."

There were also a couple of instances where people saw me at these churches, where a light bulb went on and they snapped their fingers and said, "Hey, you're Jimmy Allen's son." And I thought, "I'm not sure I can do this anymore."

In the end, though, I'd have to say it wasn't that the small "negatives" of these more traditional Churches of Christ couldn't be overcome. There were lots of positives there. It's just that Cheryl and I were ready for something different. We were late-30s, living in a new place and ready to strike out on our own. To find the place that fit us. To find the place where we wanted to be, and dare I say, where we believed God wanted us to be. And so onward we strode.

We tried two "Christian Churches." They were a lot like the Church of Christ, but with a band. We liked them okay, but neither one of them was THE ONE. At the first Christian Church, which also happened to meet in a high school auditorium, the funny-young-articulate speaker told a slightly suggestive joke. Errrrrk. We thought that was a bad sign and quickly moved on.

We broadened our horizons. There was a gigantic "Bible Church" just down the road from us. Their attendance was close to a gazillion on the weekends. Like Joel Osteen numbers, but not quite. The preacher (or pastor as these guys are mostly called) had grown up in a Jewish household and had converted to Christianity while in college. He was good. Smooth. Funny. Full of grace. We liked it there. Our kids mostly liked it there. We ended up leading a small group at this church. But, after about a year, we decided to try something else. Big churches worked for some people, but not for us. Plus, the emphasis on baptism was really small, which made me feel guilty a lot, and there were some "interesting" teachings on "Revelation" and "the end times" that I had a hard time swallowing. We liked the church, but not enough to stay. And so the church search was on again.

This time I did more research. I pulled up a list of "Willow Creek Associated Churches." We liked Willow Creek, a Chicago-area community church, although we'd never been there. We were familiar with Bill Hybels' books and John Ortberg's books and thought a church that was aligned with those guys couldn't be too bad. I also looked at the different churches' on-line doctrinal statements, mainly at the teachings on baptism in order to sooth my aching conscience. I wanted a church that strongly presented baptism as a part of what people should do. I wasn't really hung up much on other traditional Church of Christ teachings about women leading in worship, instrumental music, etc. I did prefer taking communion each Sunday, but was okay with just doing it in our own home if the church didn't offer it weekly.

The first place we tried was a community church about 20 minutes down the road with about 600 people in attendance. The church featured a slightly plump and down-to-earth "older" guy as the preacher. They met in a new building that had just opened up 2 weeks before and offered a solid foundation of grace and God-is-love. We thought, "This is it. It's perfect." (Okay, it wasn't perfect, but it was pretty close.)

And we've been there ever since.

Our daughter was baptized there. Our son was also baptized, but not there. (He chose to be immersed in the Atlantic Ocean.) Cheryl's friend was baptized there.

At this church, we lead a small group. We sometimes disagree with the senior minister. We sometimes disagree with the junior ministers. But we understand now. That's life. That's life in the Kingdom of God. This great big body of believers that stretches all the way around the world. Believers in Christ. Trying their best to please Him inside churches that fit.

What do you think? Are you okay with that?

———

Donald (b. 195X)

Years ago, if you decided to attend a denomination other than the Church of Christ, then people would say you had left THE church. In other words, you had left God.

Joe (b. 1959)

A job change took our family out of the "Bible Belt" and into an area where there was a very small group of Church of Christ members in a city of over 60,000 people. As my wife and I became more involved in the congregation there, we found an increasing tension between the role of our church in evangelizing and the seeming lack of interest by church members to carry out that vision.

At around this same time, I attended a Promise Keeper's event and was awestruck by the hearts of so many men who proudly followed Jesus Christ but who did not come from a Church of Christ background. I became curious and hungry for the passion I found in these men and was also puzzled by how casual a good number my fellow church members were—many of whom showed little emotion. I also began to notice how my local church leaders appeared to be more concerned about surface and procedural issues and less interested in issues of the heart and in reaching out to our community. So much time was spent discussing whether or not someone could clap during a song, which songbook was the "right one," and even when a service had officially ended in order for a woman to say something out loud, that it left little emotional energy to focus on our larger community who didn't know Christ. My wife and I recognized this was not true of the Church of Christ as a whole, but only of the congregation where we lived. These issues took a toll on us spiritually and physically.

Finally, our family reached a point where we felt we no longer fit in with that body of believers. With no other viable local church options, we began commuting many miles away to a Christian church that simply felt right in terms of what we believed the Bible to say and what we could "feel" when we worshipped there.

It has been many years now since that change. Our kids have been raised in a Christian church, baptized in one, and attended a Christian college (however, not a Church of Christ college). My wife and I have helped plant and grow what remains a very successful Christian church in our previous city. Our extended family is now spread between churches of Christ (running the gamut from conservative to progressive), Christian churches, and community churches. Many of our friends still attend a Church of Christ, while many others now attend other community and Christian churches. Neither my wife nor I have hard feelings toward those in our Church of Christ heritage. In fact, we very much appreciate the strong Bible teaching and Christian role models there which have provided us a solid spiritual foundation. We have simply found, though, that the freedoms we enjoy through our Christian church have allowed us to more effectively serve God.

Rebekah (b. 1971)

A few years after high school, I began dating a guy who was not raised in the Church of Christ, and I decided early on to encourage him to go to church with me. One problem was that he didn't have a fashionable suit. In fact, he owned a thick corduroy jacket with patches on the elbows, which was a terrible fashion faux pas. We got some stares from people who were considered "pillars" in that community. That was my last straw for attending the Church of Christ.

Steve (b. 1950)

I grew up in Phoenix, Arizona, and have many fond memories of people and events in the Church of Christ. My father and mother were very active, attending church just about every time the doors were open. I was taught to study the Bible from a very early age in my Bible classes there.

Even as a child, however, I was always puzzled by our exclusiveness. For example, I loved my uncle and his family, but was hindered from having a close relationship with them because they were Southern Baptists. This belief system, that we in the Church of Christ were right and everyone else was wrong, was later reinforced during my time at Harding College. As a student at Harding, I was taught that Christians were saved by grace, but that people who were wrong about any of the "big Church of Christ issues" were toast. I got the impression that God was an all-seeing eye looking down on us, ready at any second to condemn certain people to hell. My own picture of a loving God was constantly being blurred by this other depiction of a judgmental God. Being a good soldier, I stayed in the Church of Christ for the next 35 years. The last 8 of those years, while I was serving as an elder, were the most difficult for me.

Sadly during that period, as a group of elders, we spent a lot of our time keeping people "happy" and making sure the budget was not negatively impacted. There was also a guiding principle that ran through the fabric of our church, seeming to trump everything else we did. It went something like this: If a person strongly questioned any of the Church of Christ core doctrines (which had been figured out a long time ago), then it was time for that person to leave. There was no room for any thoughts outside of those core doctrines.

As an elder, I heard from a lot of people who felt unhappy with others who did not uphold Church of Christ traditions. In my view, many of these people had heart problems, but instead of teaching and shepherding them, our eldership simply acquiesced and said, "Okay, the things that bother you won't happen again." It became known that a person could treat other people harshly if he or she had the "right" doctrine. This behavior was modeled by the pulpit minister, and his actions were generally overlooked or excused by the elders. While we talked about the leading of God's spirit, it wasn't something that was widely experienced in our church. "Right doctrine" was the rule of the day, and change was not acceptable, but I began to believe positive change was needed—that transforming into the image of Christ was essential.

Our family has now spent the past two years at a nondenominational community church. Here, we have finally found a message of grace and hope, a message that puts Christ at the center and allows our trust to be in him and not in an institution. We have missed many friends, but we have been richly blessed by God each Sunday. It has been an incredible thing to worship with all of our heart, mind and soul.

Wesley (b. 1968)

Unlike a lot of my friends, I don't have any bitterness about my time in the Church of Christ. In fact, I really appreciate the emphasis on scripture. At the same time, I don't have any patience for the Church of Christ now. My view of God is much too big to be contained in that narrow doctrine. WAY too big.

You know what I miss the most about the Church of Christ, though? Singing a cappella. Strange, isn't it?

In the End

On a warm Sunday afternoon in May of 2009, I attended a reception for my dad at Harding University. He was retiring after 50 years as a member of the Harding Bible faculty. Quite a milestone. My mom and sister and brother were there along with dozens of other well-wishers.

The reception took place in the Cone Chapel, a second-floor room with glass windows overlooking Harding's front lawn ... the same lawn I used to romp on as a kid ... the same stretch of grass where I held hands and fell in love with my college sweetheart.

Harding chancellor (and our Searcy next-door neighbor) Cliff Ganus made a presentation to my parents. Dad gave a little impromptu speech. Surrounded by family and old friends, I felt a coziness in that room that I don't experience much anymore. It was a nice afternoon.

At one point mid-reception, an older couple approached me. They were parents of friends of mine, and they gave me a firm handshake and a little hug (respectively). Then Mrs. R asked me a question that I'd heard a few times before.

MRS. R: Now, Mike, are you preaching?
ME: No, ma'am. I'm not preaching.

MRS. R: Well, are you teaching a Bible class?

ME: No, ma'am. I'm not teaching a Bible class.

MRS. R: (pausing and patting me on the arm) Well, I'm sure you do your part."

At first this kind of hurt my feelings. (I'm kind of wimpy.) But later, I thought, "She's exactly right. That's what I do. I do my part. And maybe that's not such a bad thing."

Maybe God is okay with people who do their part.

———

At the end of the day, what can I say?

I can say, I grew up

    in a church

    in a family

    in a school

where people loved God and loved each other.

And I can say, It was good.

The Songs

"Be a Booster": By Ferne Winters. Public Domain.

"The B-I-B-L-E": Unknown author.

"Blest Be the Tie": By John Fawcett (1740-1817) and Hans Nageli (1773-1836). Public Domain.

"Father Abraham": Unknown author.

"For All the Saints": By William How (1823-1897) and Ralph Williams (1872-1958). Public Domain.

"God Give Us Christian Homes": By B.B. McKinney (1886-1952). Public Domain.

"Happy All the Time": By Albert Benjamin Simpson (1843-1919). Public Domain.

"If You're Happy and You Know It": Unknown author.

"Jesus is Lord" or "Alleluia": Unknown author.

"Just As I Am": By Charlotte Elliott (1789-1871) and William Bradbury (1816-1868). Public Domain.

"Love Lifted Me": By James Rowe (1865-1933) and Howard E. Smith (1863-1918). Public Domain.

"O Why Not Tonight?": By Elizabeth Reed (1794-1867) and J. Calvin Bushey (1847-1929). Public Domain.

"The Wise Man and the Foolish Man": By Hermann Voss. Public Domain.

Acknowledgments

My thanks to:

Cheryl, Kate and Cal for everything.

Mom, Dad, Cindy and Jimmy for teaching me to love God and His word in the early years.

Brian, Karen, Andrew, and Andrea for reading the manuscript and for saying nice things about it.

Old friends from the College Church of Christ, Harding Academy, Harding University, Central Arkansas Christian Schools, Pleasant Valley Church of Christ, Southwest Church of Christ, Minot Church of Christ, Brandon Church of Christ, Southgate Church of Christ, Pearl Harbor Church of Christ, Oahu Church of Christ, and the Hartford Church of Christ.

My brothers and sisters in Christ at FCC.

Jeff Montgomery for the final photo.

C.S. Lewis and Philip Yancey for inspiration along the way.

About the Author

Mike S. Allen, a graduate of Harding University with a degree in print journalism, has written articles for newspapers and military publications. He has also spoken to a number of churches around the world as a part-time youth minister, full-time assistant minister, and regular ol' church member. He is a husband, father, and friend who enjoys working and living in the Washington, DC metropolitan area (except during rush hour).

Have a story to share?

Email: cofcproject@gmail.com
Blog: growingupcofc.blogspot.com

12934595R00121

Made in the USA
Lexington, KY
05 January 2012